Saint Mary's Silver Connection

THE LOVE OF
SKIING

THE LOVE OF
SKIING

By John Samuel

Foreword by
Jean – Claude Killy

CRESCENT BOOKS

New York

Contents

© MCMLXXIX Octopus Books Limited
First English edition published 1979 by Octopus Books
Limited, 59, Grosvenor Street, London, W1

Library of Congress Catalog Card Number 78-24180
All rights reserved
This edition is published by Crescent Books,
a division of Crown Publishers, Inc.

Samuel, John, 1928–
   The love of skiing

   1. Skis and skiing. I. Title.
GV854.S2242 796.9'3 78-24180
ISBN 0-517-27341-1

Printed in Hong Kong

Endpaper
High up in the Monashee range of the Canadian Rockies.
Half-title
Climbing higher for a longer run in the powder at Verbier, Switzerland.
Title
The helicopter takes you to the top – then it's 100,000 vertical feet of powder in a week for this group.
Right:
Deep powder, bright sun, long slopes; that's the skier's dream.

Foreword

Each year, skiing becomes more popular. Why is this happening? Skiing is not cheap and hardly a lazy and comfortable form of relaxation. But for many, two weeks' skiing is the ultimate holiday. The combination of exercise and relaxation in a vital and healthy atmosphere helps make skiing a total escape from the day-to-day jobs and chores. The concentration and physical exersion needed further helps one to forget the non-skiing world. But what compels all skiers and creates the ski-bug, is the exhilaration derived from the sport. From the beginner who has just made his first stem turn to the top racer who has put in a winning run on a slalom course, the feeling of satisfaction and achievement is intense, a moment that will long be remembered. For others, skiing presents another frontier, a challenge for personal and human accomplishments – to break the 200 kph barrier in the speed trials, to perform a triple somersault with a full twist, to lay even, regular tracks in deep powder. For those who achieve these feats, the challenge continues – more speed, longer jumps, greater perfection. For those who fall short, the challenge remains, urging them on. The competitive element in skiing is important, for many of the developments in competition ultimately benefit the non-competitor. But competitor or otherwise, all skiers have one thing in common. The enjoyment and satisfaction they find in the sport, at all levels and at all ages, the challenge and the recreation, all add up to create their love of skiing and are beautifully recorded in this superb book.

JEAN-CLAUDE KILLY

Right
Jean-Claude Killy became France's hero and an international star by winning three gold medals at the Grenoble Olympics in 1968.

The History of Skiing

From caveman to superstar

As with all his love affairs, man's association with skiing has passages of quarrels, hatreds and reconciliations. The Scandinavians hated downhill skiing in the first instance, though it was a Norwegian peasant, Sondre Norheim, an epic if sad figure, whose experiments led to the modern ski shape and the fixed binding which made modern skiing styles possible.

Like all the oldest sports, skiing is founded on man's most elementary needs. Running, jumping, swimming and various forms of combat, are at the heart of the Summer Olympic Games. Similarly, skiing in all its forms is the centre of the Winter Games. In Siberia, Scandinavia, Northern China and Canada, forms of snowshoe or ski have been used since prehistory. The Hoting ski, found in a peat bog in Central Sweden, is the oldest yet discovered. It is dated around 2500 BC, made of pinewood, and is 3 ft 6 in long and six inches

wide. This short, broad type of ski is known as the Arctic Ski. A rock engraving from Rodoy, northern Norway, also of about 2500 BC, shows longer skis, and, just as interestingly, a skier apparently wearing a hunting mask, for all the world like a hare quaffing from a champagne glass. As a twentieth century image it would not do so badly.

The Romans met northern people known as Skridfinns or Skrikfinns, names used by German-speaking tribes about the non-Germanic groups of the north, Lapps and Finns. Skrika was to leap, and Diaconus, a Lombard writing in Latin in the eighth century, described how the men hunted wild animals 'by leaping forward using contrivances of wood curved like a bow'. The first printed books of the Middle Ages depicted ski troops from the Nordic countries and Russia. It was all essentially masculine and functional, the assumption being that women never left their domestic duties to slay bear, seal, deer or their fellow men.

More sporting instincts stirred in the early nineteenth century. The people of Osterdal, just north of Christiania, now called Oslo, produced a hero-athlete-comedian in Trysil Knud, who in the course of a run would snatch up pieces

Mürren, famous for its view of the Eiger, is the original home of Alpine race skiing.

of clothing, throw off a few garments or slurp from a gourd of beer. Norsemen introduced skiing to the United States, no doubt sowing the first seeds of this sort of freestyle as well as the adventurism of langrenn, or cross-country. Gullik Knedsen and the brothers Ole and Ansten Nattestad from Nymedal emigrated to Illinois to start a flourishing tradition of skiing on the Rock Prairie of Beloit, near Chicago, in 1841. Their letters home encouraged John Thorensen to emigrate from his village of Tinn, in the province of Telemark in 1838. Seventeen years later he was the only applicant for the job carrying mail over the Sierra Nevada. On 3 January 1856, he left Placerville, California, to carry the mail to Genoa, Nevada, and after an epic 90 mile trail-blazing journey he arrived three days later. The legend of 'Snow Shoe' Thomson, as he had now

become, was born. For nearly 20 years he was the human link uniting east and west of the United States by mail, because of him letters taking only 12 days to travel between San Francisco and New York instead of the three months it took by clipper round the Horn.

Thomson's skiing was straight running, wherever possible, with braking achieved by a long, stout pole held across the body and pressed into the snow. Turns were executed by stepping round, and stops by jabbing in the pole. With only a crude toepiece to attach boots, the heel flopped up and down, rendering control of the rough, flat blade-shaped ski extremely difficult. Back home, things were beginning to change, but in the most unlikely way. On 8 February 1868, a man of 43 in rough, country garb, went among the

gentlemen of Christiania at their annual ski championships at Iverslokka, and to their dismay won all four competitions – style, jumping, loipe and free running. *Aftenblad*, 10 February 1868, wrote: "Sondre Auversen Norheim from Norgedal won all four disciplines with the notation 'Outstanding'. For the 'Jump with Ski Pole' he was awarded the additional qualification of 'virtuosity'.... With a short stick in one hand, which he used rather like a walking stick, and his hat in the other, he starts his free run at very great speed, making a number of small jumps, each about two or three ski lengths clear of the snow, landing each time with the grace of a dancer and in perfect balance. Until you have seen this man, now aged 43, ski, you have not been skiing."

Sondre Auversen, or carpenter's son, adopting the Norheim from the feudal manor which sponsored him, against all tradition had defeated his social superiors, to their chagrin, with a new style of equipment married to a new technique. It was another two months before *Aftenblad* described the heel binding of twisted osiers by which Auversen anchored his heel to his ski. The ski itself, fashioned by his home-made plane, adze, saw and chisel, was revolutionary. For 10,000 years and more, people had skied on skis three metres long, crudely shaped, heavy and fixed only by a toe strap. They were barely in control of them, certainly at any kind of speed. Auversen's reputation in Morgedal was as a bad or lazy workman, a dreamer. His wife sometimes had to beg to supplement her own income from needlework and Auversen's feeble contribution. His time, however, was not being totally wasted. From his whittling

View from the Aiguille du Midi, Chamonix, to the most famous panorama in the Alps – the Grand Combin, the Matterhorn and Monte Rosa.

and his chipping came a ski of 2 m 40 cm, which was fully 60 centimetres, or two feet, shorter than the clumsy skis of the time. Not only that, he waisted the ski to 69 mm, compared with 84 at the front and 76 at the tail, in other words widths which are little changed by ski manufacturers today. The upshot were skis that, for the first time, ran straight and true, and were much more controllable for jumping and turning.

Auversen never entered another competition. In 1870, when he returned to Oslo, the competition was cancelled for lack of snow. When a ski 'factory' failed in Morgedal, Auversen emigrated to America, and he never returned. His death place is unknown, and only a slim granite memorial remains to him at Morgedal. It says, 'Sondre Auversen Norheim – Father of Modern Skiing'. To all but a few ski historians, inside and outside Norway, he is unknown.

The Telemark turn, the graceful, sweeping turn associated with Norheim's area, was the product of better ski design rather than the heel binding. Indeed the swooping Telemark turn, with its weight on the outside ski and the inside leg in the kneeling position, is utterly dependent on the heel lifting. The first man to see the possibilities of the fixed-heel technique in steeper terrain was another eccentric, Matthias Zdarsky. Zdarsky had retired to a mountain hermitage at Habernreith, near Lilienfeld in Austria to develop undisturbed his scientific and artistic ideas when he read *The First Crossing of Greenland*. He was inspired to buy a pair of skis in Norway and work out a technique with them. He quickly perceived that the fiercer angulations of his local mountains required a separate technique to that of cross-country skiing and his *Lilienfeld Skilauf-Technik (1896)* was the first serious attempt to set it on paper. While skiing with the Austrian army in World War I Zdarsky survived an avalanche in which he suffered over 70 fractures and dislocations, including six of the spine. But he came back indomitably not only to ski but to become the prophet of the new sport, a man of such Pauline intensity that he could say, 'It is the most primitive

Skiers leave the warmth and hugger-mugger of the mountain restaurant for the trails which will test their skill and their courage.

12

This drawing from an Italian book published in the Middle Ages shows Northern people of a much earlier time, probably around 800 AD, using skis to hunt and fight.

rule of conduct that of two people who have dealings with each other, one must be the speaker, the other the listener.' Zdarsky was clearly not a listener.

The Alpine pioneers found two new requirements forced upon them. Their terrain demanded that a skier traverse a slope with his ski edges keeping him from slipping, and to combine traverses in broadly opposing directions with a curved turn across the fall line, the steepest part immediately below a given point. Between 1890 and 1896, Zdarsky found ways of descending steep slopes quickly and safely in a series of curves or turns. His turn became known as the Stem Christiania, after Oslo's original name and in proper deference to skiing's Norwegian heritage. It involved basically a heel push and in German a 'beinspieltechnik', or leg play. It dominated Alpine technical thinking for the next 70 years, and elements remain in the most modern techniques, although, as with Norheim, improved physical characteristics, especially with skis and boots, have brought further radical changes of technique and instruction.

Zdarsky used a form of gate in what he termed a *torlauf* to improve technique. Racing, however, was not a special interest, and the opportunity competition gave not only to develop aggressiveness – an element essential for successful skiing – but to refine technique was being pursued most ardently by an Englishman, Arnold Lunn. He did so in a typically Edwardian British way, marrying aesthetics to Victorian pragmatism, as his father did before him. If Arnold was the father of modern Alpine ski racing, Henry was the father of the winter sports travel trade. The package

was truly a gift of God. Henry, a Methodist missionary, invalided home from India, in 1892 organised a conference to reunite a divided Christendom. He did so in Grindelwald, in the Bernese Oberland of Switzerland, for the reason, sufficient to him, that St. Bernard of Clairvaux once had a retreat there beneath the Eiger, Wetterhorn, Mönch and Jungfrau. 'At the end of the conference', he reported, as if lamenting the matter, 'I found myself £500 in profit.' Thence he went on to found a travel business, but since the upper class English of that time regarded it as 'not done' to go abroad in groups, he founded the Public Schools Alpine Sports Club. In its name he could book whole hotels at discount rates and his clientele submerge their unease in the name of their club and the certainty that they would find fellow guests of similar disposition. This club visited ten Swiss centres, among them Adelboden, Klosters, Montana, Wengen and Mürren.

In 1903, to amuse his guests, Henry Lunn arranged the Public Schools Alpine Sports Challenge Cup on the combined results of skiing, skating and tobogganing. The ski race was not exactly arduous. The Swiss course setter stuck a flag in each corner of a field and invited the competitors to walk round them. He reasoned that the British were neither sufficiently fit to climb nor adequately proficient to ski down. Eight years later three separate competitions were established, Henry Lunn persuaded Lord Roberts of Kandahar, a vice-president of the Public Schools Alpine Sports Club, to give his name to the ski event, and the first competition for the Roberts of Kandahar Challenge

Cup was organised at Montana in 1911. Thus a remote name from the Indian subcontinent came to be associated with skiing. Lord Roberts, it must be said, was no skier. Arnold Lunn, then 22, with one leg three inches shorter than the other following a recent mountaineering accident, was a spectator at what the British regard as the first downhill race in skiing history. It was a considerably more arduous race. Subsequently Arnold Lunn took the name Kandahar for the club he founded in Mürren to experiment with many forms of racing, in particular the slalom. At the same time he pursued an unwavering campaign against the opposition of the Scandinavian countries and, even, of the Swiss sporting press, for the equal recognition of downhill racing and slalom with the traditional cross-country and jumping events.

In modern times, with television and easy travel and communication making change more generally acceptable, it is perhaps hard to understand the rambling nature of those ancient feuds. Alpine ski racing was not accepted by the International Ski Federation (FIS) until 1930, and when at last downhill and slalom were introduced into the Winter Olympic Games at Garmisch-Partenkirchen in 1936 medals were only awarded for the combined results in men's and women's events and not for individual events.

For long, Scandinavia regarded itself as the true home of ski competition, just as England saw itself as the mother country of soccer. Genius for the sport, and ability to contrive and adapt, existed in many places, but change was looked upon cautiously. Norway staged the world's first ski competitions at Iverslokka in 1866 when Baekken from Honefoss won a prize after beating officers and students over a course with several small jumps. The Holmenkollen stadium and jumping hill on the outskirts of Oslo was built in 1892, and, because of the Norwegian strength in depth, competition there was considered of more consequence than International Ski Federation World Championships or Winter Olympic Games. Just as England at soccer was unprepared for the worldwide expansion of the sport after World War II, so the Scandinavians were taken by surprise when the East European countries, Japan, the Alpine countries and North America began winning ski jumping and cross-country medals, in abundance. The Nordic snow genius continues to express itself in a variety of forms. Birger Ruud, Norway's jumping champion, won the 1936 Olympic Downhill, Stein Eriksen took gold and silver in Giant Slalom and Special Slalom at the 1952 Games, and Ingemar Stenmark dominated the World Cup series of the later 1970s.

Switzerland, with Henry Lunn pro-

viding the detonator, was the first country to profit heavily from the explosion in the winter sports industry between the wars, although the Arlberg region of Austria, under the influence of Hannes Schneider, was not far behind. The Swiss, more quickly than the others, perceived the importance of uphill transport for downhill skiers. For several decades skiers were accustomed to an uphill slog, with skins strapped to their skis to prevent sliding backwards, for the joy of a brief run down. In part they were inheriting the practices of the ski mountaineer, and some of his puritanism. More exactly, they had no other choice. The Swiss were already ahead with the variety of funiculars and cog railways and, later, cable cars, installed for their summer trade. In 1934 came the major breakthrough with the Swiss engineer Constam, in conjunction with the firm of Bleichart of Zurich, patenting and then installing a rope draglift. The T-bar had arrived. Soon, the first chairlift was built, at Sun Valley, Idaho, in 1937. The first in Europe, it is claimed, was at Pustevny, near Radhosch, Czechoslovakia, in 1939. In 1944–45,

the Swiss von Roll introduced automatic coupling and uncoupling at stations. Afterwards came the gondola or bubble cars, lightweight swift-moving cabins for up to six people, and Poma drag lifts, made automatic with the individual setting them going by breaking a gate or passing a magic eye. The French were major innovators of automatic lifts. At their purpose-built resorts they much reduced queuing, the bane of skiing's great expansion.

On the slopes, the development of skiing was led by racers and people like Arnold Lunn and Hannes Schneider interested in developing new challenges and techniques for them, with equipment manufacturers constantly experimenting with materials which would do a given job better or cheaper. The British Ski Championship of 1921, at Scheidegg, Switzerland, was the first decisive break from Scandinavian national championships, still followed slavishly in the Alps with the title awarded on combined results of cross-country and jumping. The British awarded their championship on the combined result of a downhill race and a style competition, but Lunn quickly found the style aspect unsatisfactory. Downhill was a wonderful test of courage and strength, but there was surely more to skiing than that. Pairs of flags marking turning points over steeper terrain provided a much more exact test of skill and technique. Thus was the slalom born. Morgedal skiers of the previous century refined their downhill running and jumping with linked turns round bushes. This they called slalaam, from sla, meaning a smooth hill, and laam, a track down such a hill. Lunn christened his new event slalom in honour of these pioneers, and on 21 January 1922 set his first course on the practice slope at Mürren, the same Swiss village where he had drafted the original rules of downhill. Appropriately, the first World Championships in these events were held at Mürren, in 1931, although such was the conservatism of the FIS they were only recognised as such retrospectively. Lunn's snowball rolled and rolled before it became an avalanche, but this it became in the Thirties as the Alpine countries took up the sport in massive numbers. Schneider's St. Anton Ski School

Sir Arnold Lunn married aesthetics to Victorian pragmatism. He saw that racing would develop both aggression and technique. If Sir Arnold was the father of Alpine racing, his father, Henry, was the father of the winter sports travel trade.

Canada's Ken Read was one of the first successful challengers to Franz Klammer's supremacy in the downhill. Note the holes cut in the ski tips to reduce wind resistance.

developed the famous Arlberg style based on the stem Christiania turn and a notable crouch. He and Lunn collaborated to introduce the Arlberg-Kandahar, a race event for long the Blue Riband of skiing.

Eight years after the first British downhill, Austria followed suit. Fifteen years afterwards, with the 1936 Winter Olympic Games at Garmisch-Partenkirchen staging downhill and slalom for the first time, trains left Munich every two minutes and throughout the night on the eve of major competitions. Skiing finally was a major spectator attraction elsewhere than on the Holmenkollen hill.

Off the slopes another revolution was taking place – that in equipment design.

Skis have a romantic history. They inspire such passions that brilliant men have wed themselves to a particular design – and gone bankrupt rather than desert it. The Hoting ski was a plain board. Norheim's was shaped to a purpose. Kneissl, the Austrian ski manufacturers, using the expertise of their Tyrolean wood carvers at Kufstein, in 1936 came up with the laminated ski. Called the Splitkein, it had 18 wooden lamina, glued together for extra strength and resilience, compared with the two or three that had been developed hitherto. Quickly technology led the ski-makers into combinations of material which capitalised on the advantages of each other. If the wood could be layered like a sandwich, it could also be glued

together side by side, like a Neapolitan ice cream.

America established a lead with Harry and Hart Holmberg producing the first metal ski, called the Hart, in 1955, but a year later at the Cortina Winter Olympics, Kästle, another Austrian firm, stole ahead of everyone with an ash core ski. It was a lively slalom performer, less advanced than the Hart, but the right materials came together with the right man, the hip-wriggling Toni Sailer. The day of the Skiing Superstar dawned with the handsome young Kitzbüheler. He swept to victory in slalom, giant slalom and downhill with seconds to spare on the new Kästles. Overnight he became a television and film star, his equipment endorsements making small fortunes for manufacturers. The German-speaking countries had set the war behind them, a huge public was week-ending in the mountains. The great ski boom was under way.

The trains, the planes, the hotels and the equipment and clothing that set down a skier on a mountain posited another revolution – slope maintenance and grooming. In the old days you could shout 'Ready, steady, go' and people could slide and scramble down the mountain, in soft snow and ice, in whatever order they liked. Resorts quickly became mindful of the bad publicity accruing from the increasing number of accidents as the unwary tumbled into a crevasse or strayed on to an avalanche slope. On the Parsenn at Davos in the early Thirties, an Englishman named Bill Edlin built a bridge across a small ravine on the meadows, talked local farmers into removing some fences and paid schoolchildren to help clear rocks and broken branches from the tree paths. He equipped and paid for the first rescue patrol, and men armed with shovels filled in holes and flattened bumps. The principles of making and safeguarding ski trails were established. Not until after the Second World War did the Snocats and Ratracs appear which produced the manicured pistes common today. Soon, ski manufacturers were concentrating on skis suitable for the hard-packed snow of the busy resorts, and people who strayed off the beaten paths were regarded as the eccentics. That, in itself, produced a reaction, and soft snow skiing, particularly in the powder of the Rocky Mountain states, developed a cachet all its own, and people were crossing from Europe to sample it.

Quickly it became established that people growing up in snow countries were at far less risk than those taking a fortnight off from a desk. Countries who sent people to the snow were particularly sensitive to the accident problems. The Ski Club of Great Britain much encouraged the development of the safety binding in the 1930s. Thus the famous Kandahar binding came about – then a simple strap pulling the heel cable off the boot in a forward fall. As time went on bindings became much more sophisticated, providing for sideways, forward and backward release. Their increasingly sophisticated design became the biggest single factor in the reduction of accidents – not just of broken legs, but of the much commoner ligament and muscular strains which still ruined an expensive and long-anticipated holiday. The insurance industry quickly stepped

16

in, but the premiums were necessarily high. Packaging transport and hotels was only one aspect of the holiday. The additional costs of insurance, equipment purchase or hire, ski school and uphill transport proved a huge extra — at least half as much again of the basic package deal – for holidaymakers to the Alpine resorts.

Each major western country made its leap forward in a particular way. Symptomatic of America's contribution was the Head Standard, the first truly successful mass-produced metal ski. It opened up the mountains to the masses in a quite different way to the T-bar and the funicular. By the ease with which they turned on it, hundreds of thousands of semi-fit city dwellers could tackle the red runs previously denied them. The man behind it was Howard Head, a Martin aircraft engineer, a non-skier, who nonetheless could perceive that a

Left:
Switzerland was the first Alpine country to develop a winter sports industry. Instruction on the slopes of Kleine Scheidegg, Bernese Oberland, in 1934.

Below:
After ski school, the freedom of deep powder.

heavily stressed wooden structure was all wrong for skiing. Living in penury for eight years, he experimented endlessly before coming up with an I-beam principle with the top and bottom 'skins' connected by a core. The Head standard that emerged changed ski construction for all time. It had an aluminium top and bottom, plastic sides, and a core of sandwiched plywood layers set on edge. It was an American production-line job which did not have to be hand-made. It required no special care, it did not warp, and broke only under extreme stress. It was three times as flexible at the tips as a wooden ski, and turned easily in soft snow. Its one great drawback disqualified it as a racing ski. Its vibrating metal made it chatter at speed.

Others were all ready to jump in. Rossignol, with the Allais Major, produced the first successful metal racing ski. Franz Kneissl, whose firm had developed the Splitkein in the Thirties, put his money on a fibreglass casing and a young racer called Karl Schranz. The White Star became the world's number one recreational ski in place of the Head and the Allais Major, and Schranz became a world champion. Foam cores followed fibreglass, and wet-wrap, a kind of mummifying process giving different properties over the ski length, succeeded fibre sheets. Wet-wrap produced the Dynamic VR-17, and the ski produced the man — Jean-Claude Killy. A soft tip and a hard tail gave Killy just the instrument he needed for his avalement technique. With his phenomenal strength he could sit back and 'jet' out of turns. France celebrated its Grenoble Winter Games with Killy winning three gold medals and the reflected publicity shining on all the third generation, purpose-built resorts springing up between Geneva and the Mediterranean. Dynamic introduced the first plastic base, which started the process whereby waxing of Alpine skis for holidaymakers became less important. Blizzard contributed the outstanding Blizzard Epoxy. the most successful fibreglass ski of its time, and major advances were afoot in a variety of directions. Manufacturers who got too far ahead of their public, with highly priced super skis more suitable to the Hahnenkamm at Kitzbühel than 15 mph pistes, were at considerable risk. At the same time they could not afford not to be associated only with racing success. Annemarie Moser-Pröll made the Austrian manufacturer Atomic world renowned by her World Cup victories and her endorsements. Fischer owed an immense amount to Franz Klammer, with his

Olympic and World successes, before they parted.

Hot dog, the original expression for freestyle skiing, and a specific American contribution, accelerated the move into shorter, lighter Compact skis. Most skis in the Seventies were of two types, sandwich and torsion box. Short skis were always easier to handle, as the migrating northern tribes of the third millennium before Christ realised. The problem was in their stability at speed. Modern, sometimes computerised processes, produced a more stable short ski, and at one time the right height for a Compact was put at brow height. This eased up to head height, and the same processes which created the stable short ski introduced also strong yet flexible longer skis. The essential production advances were the right combination of plastic, fibreglass and metal to provide both strength and flexibility, and injection moulding of cores such as phenolic plastic. These you can shave off, chop down and variously manipulate to provide a core with constant and specific properties. Other cores are foam, foam and glass, wood and foam, and still, in some cases, just wood. Manufacturers use different substances and varying designs. Hexcel and Hart developed a honeycomb core, Dynastar an acrylic foam core with an omega-shaped fibreglass or metal reinforcing rib with metal laminates. K2 were of fibreglass with wood core, Rossignol a metal/glass foam sandwich; Yamaha had seven layers of glass. So it went on, with skis in the forefront of technological advance in the properties of laminates and cores. So, people were advised to buy according to weight, age, standard and even psychological attitude. 'Are you aggressive?', a ski shop adviser might beatle at his customer, 'Yes, but only to aggressive shop assistants,' I was once minded to say. It certainly remains true that a stiff ski holds better on hard or icy snow, and a ski with softer tips is better in light or soft snow. Good sharp edges are essential in hard conditions, but the sharpness is necessary in the 30 inches of inside edge under the foot where the turn is effectively executed. Blunt edges are better in soft snow. Associated with edge control is the direct application of weight from modern polyurethane or thermoplastic boots. George Joubert, the Grenoble professor of ski, considers modern boots to have affected technique as much or more than modern skis. Polyurethane, thermoplastic and other man-made substances have wholly replaced leather, providing a much more effective shell for strict ski-edge control.

Skiing Worldwide

The word 'ski' is almost as international as Coca-Cola

Forty-eight of the world's 175 countries are what can be termed snow nations. They are either sufficiently mountainous or of the appropriate latitude for some part of the country to expect occasional or permanent snow cover. All 48 have a national ski federation affiliated to the International Ski Federation, better known by its acronym, FIS.

Many people would start the Ski ABC with Austria because of its pioneer contribution to Alpine skiing, hundreds of ski resorts and villages, 22 funicular railways, 100 cable cars, 377 chair lifts (156 double and 221 single) and 2,075 ski tows (at the last available count). In fact the ABC of FIS begins with Algeria, continues with Andorra, Argentina, and Australia, and only then comes to Austria. While no-one can possibly depreciate Austria's unique position in the skiing pantheon, it is a worthwhile reminder that many parts of the world

Lake Placid, in up-state New York, the venue for the 1980 Winter Olympics. The skier is on Whiteface, the downhill course.

delight in the sport and have interesting places to visit. So, while the list of 48 finishes hot and strong with the United States of America, it is supported next to bottom by Turkey. Mount Ararat, on which the legend of Noah is based, after all is 16,925 feet, but as famous, and much more relevant to the skier, is Uladeg, ancient Mount Olympus, a few hours from Istanbul, with a gondola and dozens of T-bars and rope tows, the Jet Ski School and a multi-lingual Turkish set playing bridge, konken and bezik before roaring fires, and glasses of local wine, Kral or Dikmen, at their side.

The search for new places to ski goes on and on. Not only do people seek some Shangri-La in unexpected corners of the world. They experiment and adventure in their own backyards, increasingly, though, with opposition from environmentalists. Switzerland, 'discovered' as a ski country by Henry Lunn, quickly perceived the advantages of turning its spas, like St. Moritz Bad, or tubercular convalescent centres, such as Arosa and Leysin, into ski centres. Skiing once on the Piz Nair above St. Moritz Dorf with American companions, we saw a great plume of smoke from the valley. Presently we heard a hotel was alight. Next, that it was the hotel of my companions.

Racing down, we found a wing truly ablaze and a crocodile of humans passing out each other's belongings, while fire appliances tried vainly to contain it. The hotel was a centre for the Club Mediterranée, the French holiday group. All staying in it, fortunately, were uninjured because the conflagration started while they were on the slopes. A fireman paused to wipe the sweat from his brow. 'To think', he said, 'this was once the hotel of the Tsar of Russia.' Love of mountains endured while Alpine folk were content to winter in their valley villages.

No one person can know all of skiing's great 48. No Austrian would pretend to an intimate knowledge of his own country's endless kilometres of formal runs. If such a super skier, and super traveller, existed, he might only know them in one set of conditions. And as a novice skier learns in a couple of days, conditions change not just over-night but in minutes and seconds. Even in constant conditions no two runs are ever the same, just as no two golf rounds are ever identical. In skiing, the permutations are endless, which is one of the great fascinations. My Ski ABC is therefore highly personal, as everyone's must be, but helped by impressions of other skier-writers which I have found particularly vivid, interesting and valid.

I would begin, not with skis on my boots, not even with my feet on a mountainside, but on a plain above Rawalpindi at 6,000 feet, the wind soughing across the foundations of a city half buried under the dust even in Alexander the Great's time. Staring at me, even as I write, is the clay image of a Ghandara goddess I stooped to pick up from under a stone where it had lain for the thousands of years since men began to move north-west from areas such as these into the great snow belts of Siberia and fashion snow boards for themselves.

The same afternoon, up into the Himalayan foothills now, on the road to Srinigar and Kashmir, and K2, second highest mountain in the world, on the farthest horizon, snow began to fall.

Near Murree, ancient hill retreat of the British Raj, I looked in vain for signs of a ski slope, or more pertinently what might be made into a slope. 'You'll find only monkeys there,' said my good friend and guide, Zawar Hassan, pointing at an almost sheer face. The road to Kashmir was barred because of political dispute, but at Murree we stopped for tea and the courtesies that are inseparable from it. A mountain village it

The Snowy Mountains, astride Victoria and New South Wales, are Australia's most extensive mountain and snow region. Skiers at Smiggins Holes hope not to come unstuck under the gum trees.

certainly was — blue-eyed, grey-eyed, brown-eyed, almond-eyed people of the hundred and one ethnic groups that make up the Punjab and North-west Frontier, mostly in the furs and warm clothing of altitude. A ski village, no. Suddenly, in a corner of a shop selling curios, furniture and plain junk, I glimpsed a pair of skis. Modern, I suppose, they were in this context — pre-war Splitkeins with Kandahar bindings. A relic of the Raj? Of some Himalayan mountain expedition long gone? The name Kandahar is not perhaps the absurdity, the Wodehousian English joke, it sometimes seems. Snow and mountain people are curiously linked.

To have skied the Atlas mountains of Algeria is a distinction shared by few Europeans in recent times. Andorra is another story as French and Spanish alike open up the Pyrenées, more bountiful of snow even than parts of the Alps in the climatically erratic Sixties and Seventies. The fiercely independent Catalans of Andorra for long guarded their 289 square miles like a mountain fortress. They are now linked by highway to Barcelona with the Spanish government driving a tunnel just over a mile and a half long under the Sierra de Cadi. The approach from Toulouse and the French side is still twisty and arduous, and lift lines in general remain shortish at Soldeu, the main resort, and drink and tobacco tax free.

Argentina's soccer players are a good deal better known than their skiers, but the FIS honoured Bariloche with its 1977 congress. Train from Buenos Aires to the Andean centre of Bariloche takes 29 hours, coach about the same and flight a couple of hours. Of the town's 15,000 beds, 5,000 are used by skiers in a season from May to September, when internationally famous racers from the Northern Hemisphere freely mix and move as they keep the snow feel under their boots. The principal ski centre of Cerro Cathedral about 12 miles away has a well-developed lift system with two cable cars up to 6,000 feet, the peak itself at 10,000 feet, and a vertical drop long enough for FIS recognised downhill courses. There is plenty of skiing to test the expert, although anyone from the Northern Hemisphere has to blink and think about the sun in the north, and south facing slopes which hold the powder while the north-facers melt the quickest. Ridge upon ridge stretches away to Chile, and Portillo, centre for the 1966 FIS World Championships.

New Zealand shares the south Pacific ski boom and the Southern Hemisphere's characteristics of sunny north slopes and snow-retaining south faces. Skiers at Queenstown, South Island.

Over the lonely peaks, condors wheel and soar. Beneath, only wild boar and little deer, known as buda-buda, leave major imprints in the snow. It will be a long time before South American skiing loses its identity with the wilderness. Portillo hots up its skiers in July and August with a three-and-a-half hour drive from Santiago through rolling farmlands, echoing gorges and dramatic peaks. Its most famous run, Roca Jack, hosts the 200 kilometre an hour speed dices of the American Steve McKinney. The 14,000 foot mountains are steep to sheer, and even the easier runs, like the Plateau, are for advanced intermediates. The national drink, pisco sour, makes a change from scotch and rye, but Chilean and Argentinian wine are the equal of many Californian and some European vineyards.

North of the equator, AUS, in the English skiing idiom, stands first and foremost for Austria. However, the skier

who hurtled down the Val Gardena World Championship downhill into third place behind Switzerland's Bernhard Russi in 1970 bore the extra syllable of the Southern Hemisphere, Australia. Earlier the same season Milne won the Val d'Isère World Cup downhill, which at the time was about the sporting equivalent of Austria winning a cricket Test match. Milne, from Myrtleford, Victoria, in fact grew up within driving distance of some of Australia's best ski country at Thredbo, in the Australian Alps.

Australia's most extensive snowfields are in the Snowy Mountain range, astride Victoria and New South Wales, in the Kosciusko National Park. The recognition of Australia's extensive mountain and snow region is relatively new. Thredbo, Perisher Valley and Smiggin Holes have become known to many European racers seeking year-round competition and fitness. At the

Among Austria's 500 ski centres, Kitzbühel, above, and St. Anton are pre-eminent. At the base of the mighty Hahnekamm run, where each year the Kitzbühel downhill takes place, holiday skiers learn the basics on the nursery slopes.

same time, weekend ski trips from Sydney and Melbourne have become increasingly popular, creating commercial possibilities undreamed of 20 years ago. 'A billowing ocean of sharp ridges and crests and stupendous valleys rolled away at our feet to the far-off snow-capped Victorian Alps. The scenery in Mexico is grand and beautiful but to my mind there is nothing grander or more beautiful than this scene from the Roof of Australia . . .' These were the words of Sir Edgeworth David in 1907 when the range was first accessible.

Now Thredbo, at 4,450 feet, boasts 2,000 feet of vertical drop, and nearly 40 miles of trails, three chairlifts and six T-bars for a season from June to October. It has a giant slalom course recognised by FIS for the experts, and night spots to satisfy holidaymakers with energy to spare. Frozen streams, glacial lakes and gnarled gum trees complete a mountain picture which is distinctively Australian. Perisher, slightly higher, has 15 ski tows and a variety of slopes, and lodges and hotels mushroom every year. Smiggin Holes, at the entrance to Perisher Valley, boasts a T-bar with a 500 foot vertical. The name derives from a Scottish term for the shallow hole trampled by cattle around a salt lick. Other centres are Mount Buller and Falls Creek.

New Zealand, sharing the south Pacific ski boom, and the Southern Hemisphere's characteristics of sunny north slopes and snow-retaining south faces, boasts 22 ski areas on North and South Islands. A spine of mountains runs virtually the length of South Island, but the four master peaks of North Island, Ruapehu, Tukinho, Turoa and Manganui, are rapidly being opened up to club and public skiing. There is still a pioneer urge and spirit to New Zealand skiing. A plane shuttle services Tekapo, one of South Island's big three; jet helicopters land experts on the Tasman Glacier of Mount Cook for two and three mile runs; Ruapehu has an international class downhill. Just as likely, however, small groups will be setting off fully armed and prepared for a day's expedition. 'Provided the skier or his party are all extremely fit, the Nelson Ski Club's Mount Robert field offers something a little different', says the New Zealand guide. 'Skiers must undertake a two-hour walk (with gear) up to the field from the car park about 3 kilometres from the St. Arnaud township.' The rope tow is an essential aspect of New Zealand skiing. So is a hardy, cheerful spirit – and by every account there is plenty of that. It is European skiing of the Thirties.

Austria long ago cast off the Thirties image, but no other Alpine country embraces skiing more in heart and mind. Switzerland geologically dominates the Alps. Austria lies to her side with relaxed, feline beauty, her peaks glittering diamond-like above her emerald forests. Her Alpine vertebrae slide gently down to the plains of Hungary. The best known – and much of the best – skiing lies in the western provinces, from the Vorarlberg in the extreme tip, eastwards over the Arlberg pass into Tyrolia, into Salzburg, Upper Austria and Styria. For the car-borne or the adventurous, there are marvellously untouched places still. In general the runs get shorter and the snow less reliable as you move east, and ski touring, or ski wandern, becomes increasingly possible.

Austria has about 500 ski centres, all but 100 in the Western and Central provinces of the Vorarlberg, Tyrolia, Salzburg, Upper and Lower Austria and Styria. The majority are set in the valleys where the farming communities first settled them. All have in common the veranda'd pitch-roofed chalet, but similarity often ends there. A keen architectural eye discerns notable differences from among the Rhaetians, Walsers, Illyrians and Germanic tribes who settled the western areas in the Middle Ages, creating the alms, or high meadows, which so often serve now as

The Matterhorn, at 14,704 feet, is 1,068 feet lower than Mont Blanc, the highest mountain of the Alps, but as an Alpine trademark it has no equal. In earlier times people believed that the souls of the dead lived in a ruined city on its summit. Superstition and legend were a form of safety device, keeping children and the foolhardy away from mountain dangers.

wide, well-kept, enticing ski slopes.

Towed along by the German mark, Austria is not the cheap tourists' paradise it was for 20 years after the War, and certainly among the British has lost out heavily to Italy in recent years. However, the German custom has multiplied, and some of the more popular centres are hard put to keep down the ski queues, especially at village level. Kitzbühel and St. Anton are examples. Once up among the miles of runs on the Horn and Hahnenkamm of the Kitzbüheler Alpen, or the Galzig or Valluga above St. Anton, there is escape. These two famous centres can be overwhelming for the beginner or novice, although the St. Anton ski school justifiably claims to be the most famous in the world. Night life teems, whether at the Tenne's kaleidoscopic amphitheatre in Kitzbühel or in *Gemutlichkeit* drinks at the Rosanna Stuberl in St. Anton.

Alpbach and Serfaus, Lech and Brandt, Ischgl and Zürs — it is impossible to do full justice to the variety of Austrian skiing. I must speak kindly of the Montafon valley in the Vorarlberg, and the pleasingly natural villages of Schruns, Tschagguns and Gargellen, and the lively charm of Seefeld, up a switchback road north of Innsbruck, where cross-country skiers loop in and out among their Alpine brethren to everyone's mutual pleasure. Spontaneity, a gift for enjoying the moment, and a willingness to please, characterise much that is best of Austrian village life. To it must be added foaming steins of good beer, cheerful light wines, and a gift for cream cake that can defy the most disciplined of weight watchers.

It is difficult to segregate exactly the Alpine countries, for so much in style, language and architecture overlaps. Switzerland's distinctive German, French and Romansch based cultures have much in common with their immediate neighbours, yet there is still a solid, stolid identity. Swiss skiing, customs and hospitality are notably different. Austria proliferates in medium runs of about 1,000 metres. Switzerland provides truly big skiing, at Davos, St. Moritz, Wengen-Grindelwald, and Zermatt, and a hotel professionalism unmatched by any. Swiss weather can be truly severe, especially in the great peaks of the Bernese Oberland and the Pennine and Leponine Alps. In the west, the cantons of Berne and Vaud provide rolling, wooded hills and pleasant, family skiing. In the south-east, St. Moritz looks south to the Italian border and a skyline of Mediterranean tints. It is still a place of style and adventure.

Above:
The Val d'Isère-Tignes area.
Below:
Les Arcs.
French resorts are of three main generations. The French mass public discovered skiing relatively late, but then the national genius produced a style of resort like no other in the world — purpose-built in the high snows.

Books can be written about its Cresta toboggan run, Bob run, curling, ballooning, ice skating, horse racing, Palace Hotel, Kings bar, gossip, scandal – and barely mention skiing. In fact the runs beneath Piz Nair and the Corvatsch have hosted Olympic Games and World Championships. It is no effete playground to the vigorous skier, but a challenge of imperial proportions. St. Moritz, truly, is the Queen of the Alps. Zermatt, beneath the Matterhorn, a prince. Swiss tourism has suffered from its strong currency, but it is often overlooked that holidaymakers are not buying domestic inflation, as they are in many other Western countries. Swiss prices have remained stable, or indeed been reduced to try to maintain a competitive position. A quarter of the country is unproductive, agriculturally, but its mountain scenery must remain as productive as watch-making and machine tools. A winter holiday in Switzerland is as relaxing and orderly as a ride in a comfortable, well-engineered car. The Swiss pride themselves on offering value for the large amount of money a ski vacation there will cost.

Which resort, then, is king? Some French might nominate Chamonix, which staged the first Winter Games in 1924. Skiers in any winter may believe their weather is exceptional. The record of the Winter Games shows that all major resorts can suffer disruption either with too much or too little. On 23 December 1924, not a flake of snow had fallen in Chamonix. Next morning there was a layer over a metre deep. Chamonix primarily grew as a mountaineering resort, dominated as it is by the Mont Blanc massif. Three huge ski areas are served by swift téléférique systems. The Brevent area lift swings nearly 5,000 feet up to its cliff top with aerial views of the runs which stir the blood of the most experienced skier. The Flégère area to the north offers another complex, while a third, the Aiguille du Midi, opens up on one of the greatest glacier runs in the world, La Vallée Blanche. The Aiguille du Midi téléférique remains one of the great mountaineering engineering feats of all time. One of the four pylons of the lower section is 170 feet high. The upper section cable, almost three kilometres long, swings near vertical up the rock face of the Piton Nord. The viewpoints over the immense glacier fields of the Mont Blanc massif are unmatched in the Alps.

France's resorts are of three main generations, but such is the rate of expansion that a fourth in the Pyrenées is emerging for the late Seventies and Eighties. The French mass public discovered skiing relatively late. When it did, the national genius for civil engineering and the relating of need to function produced a style of resort unlike any in the world. Courchevel, after World War II, was collectively planned, but followed conventional ski resort lines, with traffic, pedestrians and skiers mixed; the lessons of Zermatt, Mürren and Wengen, where nature had restricted the car, had not been learned. Likewise, Val d'Isère, Tignes and Alpe d'Huez, other second-generation resorts,

There is no more beautiful sight in the Alps than the sun on jagged, precipitous Dolomite peaks, Italy's pride and joy. Iron elements in the limestone magnesia rock create a pinkish glow. View above Selva, South Tyrol.

set high in snow productive areas, with plenty of purpose-built flat complexes, but tending to sprawl.

Then came the third generation, among them Flaine, Avoriaz, Pra-Loup, Les Arcs, Isola 2000 and La Plagne, and a hard sell which introduced a major tourist trade. France brought in the automatic tows which significantly reduced queues as well as manning costs. France introduced the short ski method to Europe. There is little *gemutlichkeit* in a French resort, but eating remains a serious, civilised business even at 7,000 feet. Runs are semi-deserted in the lunch hour and a half. Night life is disco orientated and expensive. It has little of the stomping, friendly, extrovert fun of the Austrian stübi. The French let you alone to enjoy yourself as you please; after all, they introduced the entire holiday concept to the world.

The enduringly hard Swiss franc in the Seventies made its French sister seem almost a bargain. But no country culled such a windfall as Italy, though skiers from Northern Europe only slowly began to appreciate that the country they associated most with sun, sea and indolent Mediterranean ways in fact possessed two-thirds of the Alps. Travellers from Northern Europe were also deterred by the difficulties of actually getting there. Car journeys via the German autobahns looked easy enough. But to east and west south of the Brenner Pass the tornante of the Italian mountain road, especially in midwinter, doubled or trebled the normal journey time for such a distance. Flights to Milan and Turin often are delayed by the fogs of the Po flood plain and the coach or car journey north past the lakes and into the mountain river valleys can take many hours before the resort is reached. All the same, Italy was claiming over 50 per cent of British tourists by the late 1970s and many East Coast Americans. Most Italians happily ski their well-manicured, well-mechanised *pistas*, which keep Italy's accident figures well below the average. Italy's half-time break is as ample as any . . . Campari, Chianti, Valtellina, or any one of the immense variety of Italian wines accompanying pasta and veal in equal variety. Families and children abound, especially at weekends, but Italians from the big cities keep a sharp ear and eye for the weather. A metre of soft snow and you've probably got it to yourself. Their love is the ski beach.

Italian skiing is much bigger than its reputation, in spite of the World Cup triumphs of such as Gustavo Thoeni and Piero Gros. It is in five main sections, Western Alps (Sestriere, Sauze d'Oulx, Claviere, Courmayeur, Cervinia, Macugnaga), Central Alps (Aprica, Bormio, Livigno, Madesimo, Santa Caterina), Dolomites (Cortina, Corvara, Madonna di Campiglio, Ortisei, Selva), Eastern Alps (Levico, Mecesine, Merano, Riva del Garda, Prato), and the Apennines (Abetone, Frassinoro, Campo Felice). There is no more beautiful sight in the Alps than a late afternoon sun on the jagged precipitous Dolomite peaks. Iron elements in the limestone magnesia rock create a lustrous pinkish glow – one of

Right:
Norwegians use cross-country skis to tour forests and mountains, much lower than those of the Alps, with a treeline at 3,000 feet or less.
Below:
Shared by France and Spain, the Pyrenées, although geologically older than the Alps are much newer in the skiing scene.

the wonders of the mountain world.

Spain shares its main skiing area, the Pyrenées, with France. From the Mediterranean to the Atlantic, the Pyrenées provide skiing of considerable interest and variety reliably from December until the end of March. The range is much bigger than many appreciate – 250 miles long, over sixty miles wide, and still at an early stage of their ski development. King Alfonso of Spain, we are reliably informed, skied in the Pyrenées in 1908 and the French Ski Championships took place at Peyolle, near Bagnares, as far back as 1908. The French claim about 50 resorts, chief among them La Mongie, Les Cauterets, St Lary and La Gourette, and the Spanish rather fewer, the principal centres being Baqueira Beret, Cerler,

Formigal, La Molina, Masella and Panti-cosa. Runs are fairly open, mostly above the treeline, and primarily for the beginner to intermediate at 4,500 to 7,000 feet. Some of the modern developments have been criticised for their functionalism, and après ski life is sparse compared with Austria or Italy, but Spanish drinks prices are a bargain, and resorts such as Masella and Baqueira Beret are wearing themselves in. Spain boasts about a million skiers. Some ski the Navecerrada to the north of Madrid, but the main complex south of the Pyrenées, in the Sierra Nevada, is the most southerly in Europe. It is Sol y Nieve, just north of Granada. Here Veleta and Mulhacen reach up to 10,000 feet in stark outline. Skiing here has a remarkably late season, sometimes up to

June, and it is possible, just about, to ski Spanish powder in the morning, jump into a car, motor the 90 miles and swim or water slalom in the Mediterranean by late afternoon.

In strict geographical and historic contrast, Norway, the most northerly European nation, provides the vacationer with unending vistas of snow from beginning to end of its long winter.

Scandinavia and Siberia are the home of skiing, an activity in Norway, Sweden, Finland and Russia as natural as walking or swimming, and to many needing no more precise definition. Ski touring requires no fancy names. It is walking on skis, an activity to stir an appetite before lunch or to fetch provisions from the village shop. People in exaggerated Alpine ski fashions may

feel a trifle conspicuous in Bergen, Kristiansand or Gothenburg, the subject of a slightly amused gaze. Scandinavian mountains are geologically old, rounded massifs, rising from the Norwegian fjords like leviathans. Much skiing is accomplished through forests and around lakes, among the 1,000 square miles of Oslomarka, the natural park girding Oslo, in the rolling hills of places like Varmland, Sweden, in the reindeer forests and tundra of Lapland, shared by all three countries, in the seemingly endless distances of this vast land mass. East across the Finnish border, into Russia and Siberia, well over seven million Soviet citizens are members of ski clubs. It is an activity second only to ball games in public participation. Moscow Ski Club's first event was held on January 28, 1896. Russians are especially strong in biathlon, which combines cross-country racing with shooting, and derives from

ancient hunting practices. The Russians made their Olympic debut in 1952 and at once showed what a challenge they could make to the Scandinavians in cross country, biathlon and jumping. The number of Russian women who ski was reflected in their almost immediate domination of women's cross-country events, with outstanding champions like Galina Kulakova showing that people could excel well into their thirties.

Russia has developed its Alpine skiing belatedly, and principally in one centre, Cheget, in the Mount Elbrus National Park area of the Caucasus. Cheget and Terskol are on the timberline (6,000 feet) with about a dozen hotels scattered among the pines. Open-air markets sell sweaters and sheepskin, and instead of Coca Cola and Rossignol posters there are pictures of Lenin and Marx. However, vodka is at least as good as schnapps for keeping skiers warm. The Caucasus are 600 miles long and 50

miles wide, with Elbrus at 18,510 feet and Ushba, the senior of some classic mountaineering, the Dombai, Bizengi Wall and Kasbek.

In comparison, Norway has eight formal Alpine centres – that is, resorts with sufficient vertical drop to boast FIS recognised slalom and giant slalom slopes – while Sweden offers Are and a multitude of slalom hills. Norway, Sweden and Finland make much of their winter facilities for foreign tourists, and are best visited between February and March when the days are longer. Norway's tallest peak, the Galdhoppigen, is 7,000 feet, compared with Mont Blanc, the highest in the Alps, at 15,771. The northerly latitude ensures more snow but a lower treeline – 3,000 feet or less. Arctic winds may bring weather of great ferocity, but Norway is warmed by the Gulf Stream, and Scandinavian high-pressure zones are a notable feature, bringing a light so clear that snow glitters like diamonds and colours are wonderfully enhanced. A Norwegian vertical drop of 700 feet – the qualification for an Alpine centre – gives much longer runs than its Alpine equivalent because slopes are more gentle. The great experience of Norwegian skiing, however, is in its touring skiing, up into the Vidda wilderness, far removed from city clutter and pollution. Ski hotels are subtly built to overlook such vistas, but the majority of Norwegians are content with refuge or touring huts, which provide simple but adequate facilities for their wandering.

Sweden staged the world Nordic Ski Championships at Falun in 1954 and 1974, Finland the same at Lahti in 1976, and nowhere is there a more avid watching and participating public. The annual Vasa cross-country race from Mora, 50 miles from Falun, attracts 11,000 starters for its 50 miles. Half of

Sweden's population is within a radius of 150 miles of this area, a place of undulating hills, dales and lakes with plentiful accommodation for the touring skier. Are, Sweden's principal Alpine centre, is dominated by Areskutan, at 4,500 feet, a mountain of bald, bold contours with 19 lifts and the capacity of a downhill run of two miles.

Bulgaria, Czechoslovakia, Rumania, Poland and Yugoslavia all provide Alpine skiing facilities among the Carpathian, Transylvanian, Balkan and, in the case of Yugoslavia, Alpine and Dinaric Alpine ranges. Yugoslavia has a well-developed tourist industry and regularly hosts World Cup ski races at Maribor and Kranjska Gora. As hosts of the 1984 Winter Olympic Games at Sarajevo, Yugoslavia have impressed their skiing status even more securely.

Britain's colonialism at one time came preciously close to a take-over of

the Swiss mountains. Her eighteenth
century mountaineers were followed by
racing clubs setting up shop in Mürren,
Klosters, Andermatt, Wengen and other
places, the Lunns introducing package
holidaymaking and racing styles and
rules, and the Arlberg-Kandahar races
becoming the Blue Riband of the Alps.
To those envious or annoyed by her
opportunism, she was a ski country
without the decency of her own snow
raiment. Where is your British skiing,
they could fairly ask.

The nakedness has now been covered
– in the first instance by a sporran, in the
second by man-made fibre. British love
of snow skiing can now be expressed
with a weekend coach journey from
London avoiding the hazard of a winter
Channel crossing, by a half hour's flight
from London to Aberdeen, or a car
journey of an hour to three hours from
Edinburgh or Glasgow. Since 1950 the
Scottish snow scene has been revolutionised. There are three main centres –
the Cairngorms in the Central Highlands,

Glencoe, 78 miles north of Glasgow, and
Glenshee, 55 miles north of Edinburgh.
The last two are primarily weekend
centres. Cairngorm's eleven tows, on
the other hand, can cope with 8,000
skiers an hour. Half a dozen black and
four red runs test the most expert, while
easier trails follow the yellow and green
signs for several miles of Coire na Ciste,
the White Lady and Coire Cas beneath
the 4,000-foot summit of Cairngorm. At
this latitude 100 feet of vertical is the
equivalent of 1,000 feet in the Alps. The
freezing level is the all-important guide
to skiers, with temperate south-wester-
lies likely to switch suddenly to bitter
Arctic. It is skiing for hardy folks in
December and January, but the main
season of February to April can provide
excellent runs in the protected snow-
retaining corries, or valleys. Snow conservation has been developed to a fine
art with miles of fencing retaining good
cover even for exposed sections of runs.

Scotland has its own brand of après-
ski – primarily the British pub life of the

Aviemore Centre, the custom built base village, in the cosy, hugger-mugger hotels of the granite towns and villages of Speyside, or in hotels like the Coylumbridge, or Post House, built with views of semi-wilderness.

In the beginning, God created Man. Soon after that must have come Sun, and not long after that Snow. Millions of years later, the USA created the ski resort. Americans vacationing in the Alps liked what they saw, but lacking the know-how to transport an Austrian village intact, as they were subsequently to transport London Bridge to Arizona, they brought over the Austrians handy with ski ideas and tools to an Idaho sheep pasture, just north of Ketchum. Here, Count Felix Schaffgotsch, an Austrian expert commissioned by W. Averell Harriman, found his ideal – the

sun-washed, treeless slopes of Mount Baldy. The Union Pacific Railway, Mr. Harriman's company, wrote the cheque, and in 1936–37 Sun Valley gushed, the first purpose-built ski resort in North America. It became a haunt of film stars by the score, and in later year's Ernest Hemingway's home overlooked it. Glenn Miller and Hollywood set it to music in 'Sun Valley Serenade', but the war threat scotched its early growth and most of the Austrians returned to fight in World War II. Although 'The Valley' early on produced racers such as Gretchen Frazer and Ernie McCullouch, its development post-war was more than matched by two other Rocky Mountain ski emporia, Aspen and Vail, and Mammoth, California.

Sun Valley remains the Grande Dame of US skiing. No-one tramples

Baldy without knowing he's skied one of the great runs of North America. The true ski boom struck in the Fifties with the development of the Rockies and the selling of Squaw Valley, a Californian wilderness site, to the International Olympic Committee for the 1960 Winter Olympic Games by a one-man band, Alexander Cushing. It was boosted by new and mighty snow-making weaponry which flake by artificial flake produced a reliable snow carpet for the lumpy, bumpy lower altitude East Coast centres. The snow rush brought a bigger return for Rocky Mountain and Sierra Nevada fortune hunters than gold. Until the

This is 'Steep Mother' in the Monashees. What else?

conservationists, led by the Sierra Club, began to fight back, development possibilities seemed endless. In 1977 20th Century-Fox bought the Aspen Skiing Corporation, America's largest, for $50 million, far the largest deal in the history of skiing, with the assertion that they believed ski development had a long way to go in spite of current restrictions. Colorado's governor, Dick Lamm, mindful of the pressures which forced Denver to give up the 1976 Winter Games, created a Winter Sports Council to try and balance development and conservation forces. The East were made equally mindful of the pro and con forces at work with Lake Placid going through a variety of hoops for their 1980 Olympic Games plans. Skiers in themselves do not pollute, it was argued, but the transport and victualling services

they require much change the nature of a mountain area. In the 1970s, America's ski development plans obviously were going through a sieve undreamed by people like Billy Fiske, skier and Cresta Run rider, later to die as a Battle of Britain pilot, who dreamed up Aspen in the late Thirties.

Aspen, the king of US resorts, was a semi-derelict mining town of 400 souls when Fiske and Ted and Joe Ryan had their first inspiration for a ski centre in 1936. Aspen's first lift, the 'boat tow', was rigged from mine parts. A ride cost ten cents. One ski ambition succeeded another – Aspen Mountain, Aspen Highlands, Buttermilk/Tiehack and Snowmass now provide four giant areas for up to 15,000 skiers in high season. Aspen preserves its Victorian façade for an almost Reno-like day and night

life, but its wonder is its superb powder snow. The Southern Rockies, including the resorts of Aspen, Vail, Steamboat Springs, Breckenridge, Copper Mountain, Keystone and Taos, have achieved a worldwide fame for sunshine, snowfall, low humidity, the whole combining for the famous powder.

One of skiing's ultimate experiences – helicopter skiing in the Cariboo range of the Canadian Rockies. There are no lifts, no trails. Just miles of untouched powder and thousands of vertical feet.

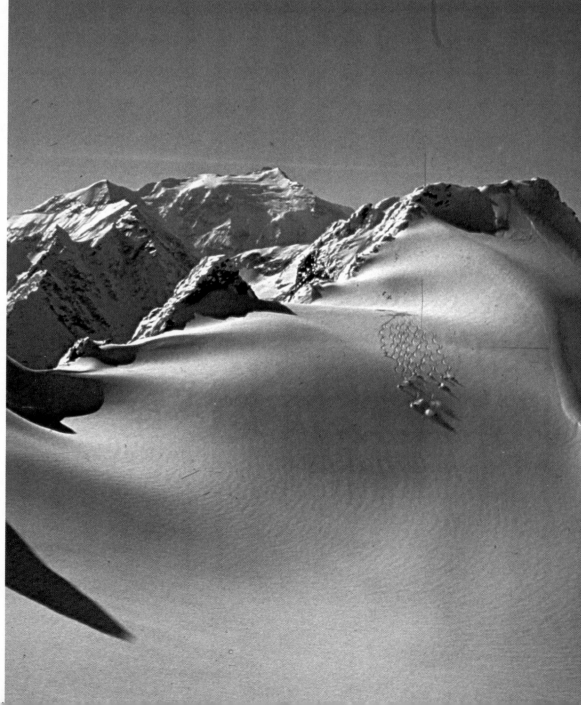

At the Continental Divide, where a stream here flows into the Gulf of Mexico, another there into the Pacific, sea is so far removed that a flake falls without a hint of salt or heaviness. More than 50 peaks in this vast area are over 14,000 feet, and people sometimes suffer sleeplessness at the seven to eight thousand feet of the resorts. But all this is secondary to the delight of easy-turning skis in the silky, thistle-down powder. More than seven million lift tickets were sold in Colorado and New Mexico in 1977–78, a success story which shows no signs of flagging. Vail, named after highways state super-intendent Charles E. Vail, who pioneered Highway 6 over Loveland and Vail passes just before World War II, was a sheep meadow in 1962. Peter Seibert, veteran of the 10th Mountain Infantry Division, earmarked it for development, and Vail Associates was born. Its architecture, unlike Aspen's, was Euro-pean influenced. Its reputation was helped by famous men such as Gerry Ford and the Kennedys, the whole combining to give it a deceptive middle-aged image. Vail's ten square miles of ski terrain do include excellent inter-mediate slopes, but its back bowls and moguls will challenge skiers of any standard. Colorado skiing is so vast it cannot readily be categorised, but longish-lasting powder is a factor com-mon both to the Southern Rockies and the Northern (Idaho, Montana and Wyoming), and in particular the resorts of Alta, Snowbird, Park City, Jackson Hole, Sun Valley and Big Sky. Snow-bird's base area is a futuristic glass and concrete piazza; Jackson Hole favours cowboy bars.

To the south-west the major resorts of the Sierra Nevada are clustered around the waters of Lake Tahoe and on Mammoth Mountain, 130 miles south, a favourite weekend site for Los Angeles ski nuts. Mammoth is sited on a dor-mant, 11,500 foot volcano, which last erupted around 40,000 years ago ac-cording to experts. Hot springs and sulphurous clouds issue from its fissures. To skiers it represents a vertical of 2,800 feet, huge treeless bowls superbly groomed for every grade, and a series of vertiginous chutes to satisfy the expert. The area was developed by one of American skiing's greatest names, Dave McCoy. Two other giant areas here

Colorado powder – it's deep, light and soft. And beautiful to ski.

are Heavenly Valley, partly in California and partly in Nevada, and Squaw Valley, on the north shore of Tahoe. The season here lasts to June. Up in the Pacific Northwest the Cascade range weather is a good deal less reliable. Sometimes it rains in January; at others houses are buried almost up to their roofs. Crystal Mountain, Washington, and Mount Bachelor, Oregon, are the principal resorts, and although most skiers are local or from Seattle the area is gradually drawing more out-of-state visitors. To the north, Vancouver offers a sail, sea and ski vista from January to April, with temperate sea winds keeping lower levels green and gentle even in winter, but sudden storms dumping huge snow deposits on local mountains like Grouse and Seymour, and, 30 miles north, Whistler Mountain. Whistler, with a vertical of 4,280 feet, has some of the longest, most challenging runs in North America. A European skier has to train up his legs for the nonstop two and three milers he can get in here.

The ski trail east leads over the Coastal range to the Canadian Rockies and another huge, largely undiscovered treasure trove of ski experience. Flying east from Vancouver the peaks reach up in vast serries. There is no sign of a trail or a house for mile upon endless mile. In the eastern sector of the Rockies, Jasper, Lake Louise and Banff are the centres for the latest craze, helicopter skiing. Here in the virgin powder of the Monashees, Cariboos, Bugaboos, Purcess and Bobby Burns ranges, helicopters set you down – at a price – for some of the purest, away-from-it skiing available anywhere in the world. Skiers, ideally of the same standard, are split into four groups of nine to twelve, plus guide with a short-wave radio. Canadian Mountain Holidays guarantee 30,500 vertical metres in a week's skiing, but you have to be fit, and a reasonably proficent skier, to get the best out of it.

East again, and the mountain scene of the Canadian Shield in Ontario, in the Laurentians north of Montreal, and at Mont St. Anne, Quebec, is sophisticated and relatively developed. The far west is young, sporty, and totally natural, its après ski restricted to a few scattered hotel bars with the occasional dance, its lighter snow and lengthy runs at once a pleasure and a challenge to the legs. Whistler is peopled more by bears,

Above:
It's downhill all the way.

Below:
Ski touring under Mount Hale, in the High Sierras.

Left and Right:
*Japan is a late but fanatically enthusiastic
convert to skiing. Sapporo, on the most
northerly island of Hokkaido, hosted the
1972 Winter Olympic Games. Visitors are
at once struck by the volcanic nature of
Japan's mountains and the hot springs
and steam clouds issuing from the
fissures.*

with some newfangled Norwegian skis
he had acquired, some snowshoes and
toboggans. It slowly grew from there.
Some local boosters lobbied and gained,
to their own surprise, the 1932 Winter
Olympic Games. Europeans laughed
when Lake Placid, altitude 1,862 feet,
had to haul in snow from Canada to
help repair the cross-country tracks.
Winter sports resorts throughout the
world came to respect the need for
artificial snow, pioneered in America in
later years. Vermont was truly the first
US ski state, with trails laid out by
President Roosevelt's Civilian Conservation Corps, mainly drawn from the
Depression unemployed, under Charles
Lord, a construction engineer employed
by the chief state forester, Perry Merrill.

Rainstorms followed by sub-zero
temperatures and glare ice are conditions all too familar to New Englanders.
Snowmaking and grooming have lost
them a little of their character-building
reputation. Equally, cross-country skiing has boosted their appeal. Trail maps
and pictures of New England centres
still look like X-rays of a difficult heart
condition, but the mini-vacation is
beginning to vie with the weekend trip
in New England Lodges and hotels. The
main centres are Hunter, Mount Snow,
Killington, Stratton, Bromley, Sugar-
bush and Stowe. Vermont offers more
centres than New Hampshire, but Sugar-
loaf, in north-western Pennsylvania,
remains northern skiing. Down south
there are many happy southerners
sporting in the snow, artificial or otherwise. Snowshoe, West Virginia, and
Beech and Sugar Mountains, North
Carolina, have ski amenities. The last
two are in a dry county, so private club
membership is necessary for skiers who
like to be wet inside as well.

Japan is a relative newcomer to
holiday skiing, indeed to the entire holiday concept, but, as with so many other
leisure aspects, has quickly made up for
lost time. In fact her ski history is an old,
if not ancient, one. Eighty-three years
ago a Captain Matsukawa first brought
skis from Scandinavia, then in 1906 a
Mr Delmailand Keif, a military attaché
at the British embassy, donated skis to
an army regiment in Sapporo. The first

racoons and marmots than human
beings. The whistling out east is more
likely to come from coachloads of
American teenagers, many of them a
trifle culture shocked at the Gallic
qualities of Quebec or the Anglicised
habits of Ottawa. The sports editor of a
distinguished American newspaper was
shocked to find a waitress totally un-
comprehending of an English breakfast
order at a ski inn near Owl's Head, a few
miles from the US border in the Eastern
township region.

Quebec province is enormous: like
British Columbia in the west, it is as
large as Western Europe. Where Quebec
offers Mont St Anne and a few other
less elaborate hills primarily as city
facilities, the Upper Laurentian Area on
Autoroute 15, between 40 and 100 miles
north of Montreal, soaks up weekender
and weekly vacationer alike, so diverse
are the resorts. Tremblant, in the far
north, can become heavily crowded on
a fine weekend. With 2,200 feet of
vertical descent, and snow-making to
help with any natural deficiency, Tremblant has justified much of the expecta-
tion of the eccentric Irish-American
millionaire Joe Ryan, who helped Fiske
develop Sun Valley. Ryan installed here
the second chairlift in North America

and just before the war played host at
Tremblant Lodge to guests like Norma
Shearer, Tyrone Power and Lionel Barry-
more, among the first Hollywood stars
to give this brand new sport of skiing
some glamour and bravura.

The Eastern Townships, an hour
and a half's drive south-east of Montreal,
provide the first sample of Appalachian
skiing. The whole area has a sense of
historical romance. It was the country
of Indian wars, Rogers' Rangers, and
the dividing line for rebels and loyalists
in the War of Independence. The British
after a while gravitated to the towns,
leaving the French to carve out farms
from the wilderness. Geologically it is
fascinating, with huge, isolated mountains of hard rock rising like leviathans
from a calm sea. Orford and Jay Peak,
just over the US border, are more
formally part of the chain which sweeps
far south into the temperate regions of
the USA. Not far over the border lies
Lake Placid, the 1980 Games centre, and
Whiteface mountain, its 3,178 foot vertical the highest in the East. The village
was one of the first in America to
establish winter sports as a vacation
idea. Melvil Dewey, organiser of the
Lake Placid Club, decided in 1904 to
keep the club open through the winter

All Japan Ski Championships were held in 1923 and two years later the Ski Association of Japan was formed.

Her ski equipment industry has leapt forward in the last decade, and a Winter Olympic Games was hosted at Sapporo in 1972 with outstanding success. The Japanese have quickly excelled in jumping; indeed they won all three medals in the Games 70 metres. Sapporo, on Hokkaido, the most northerly island of Japan, has grown from a sparse settlement to a city of a million in a hundred years. Its outlay of $555,556,000 for the Games had implications over and above ten days of snow and ice sport. Sapporo was anxious to establish itself in world eyes, and to millions of Japanese, looking for new ways to enjoy their increasing money and leisure, as a ski centre. Sapporo has long been famous for its Snow Sculpture Festival in Otaru Park, with legendary creatures sculpted in snow and ice, and beautiful flowers preserved in showcases of diamond and ice — all there and gone in a few days.

By the same token, Mount Eniwa, a virgin mountain of 4,000 feet, a pyramid of glittering birches, was manipulated by 15,000 men, 850 bulldozers and six tons of explosives for two downhill races, the men's and women's, and accoutred with two cable cars and a chair lift. As if by magic wand, it was then returned to its pristine state, as required by the conservation laws, within a few weeks of the end of the Games. Japan's point was made. She was a major ski power. Teine Highland, with 13 lifts and night illumination, centre for the Olympic slaloms, is primarily served by Sapporo, under an hour's journey away. Furano, an hour further away, in 1977 and 78 staged World Cup competition events. Hokkaido is subject to violent changes of weather with the juxtaposition of the Siberian high- and Pacific low-pressure weather systems. Japan's vast volcanic mountain necklace stretches 1,000 miles from latitude 30 to latitude 45, and plenty of skiing is possible within reach of major cities. Mount Fuji, 12,272 feet, Japan's highest and most beautiful mountain, sacred to the Shinto religion which worships nature, is visible on a clear day from Tokyo. Skiers of all grades may sport around its lower slopes and lakes, but a descent from the sacred summit is only for a super skier such as the Japanese national hero Yichiro Miura, (see The man who skied Everest). The story is told by the American Eric Perlman, the first non-Japanese to ski Fuji from the top, that on reaching the weather and radar station, perched on the crater lip, after a particularly perilous Easter climb with Miura, they opened the door to find the crew playing Mah-Jong — or watching lady wrestlers on TV.

Naeba, 2 hours 20 minutes by express train from Tokyo, staged a World Cup event in 1975, and with a season from mid-December to early May, a little longer than the usual for Japan, boasts 27 lifts and two hotels. Kusatsu, Manza, Joetsa, Kokusai, Iwappara, Nakazato, Ischiuchi and Nikko Vumoto are other centres within reasonable distance of the capital. Most have night illumination and hot springs. The Japanese bath ritual is not least of the apres ski delights of Japan, a cleansing of spirit as body, and if these comforts are not enough there is always saki, and excellent wines, whiskies and beers, for the thirsty skier.

The White and the Weather

Snow, the tiger in lamb's clothing

Matthias Zdarsky was not only a pioneer of skiing techniques, he was able to express himself. 'Snow', he wrote, 'is not a wolf in sheep's clothing. It is a tiger in lamb's clothing.' Like the tiger, it is a beautiful thing, but when it is hungry, wounded, or treated with disrespect, it is ruthless and unpitying. In the 1964 Winter Olympic Games at Innsbruck I remember two attractive young competitors, the American Bud Werner and West German Barbi Henneberger. It was a considerable shock to learn of their deaths just two months later in an avalanche in the notorious Val Selin near St. Moritz. They were part of a group filming in the area. They ignored several closed notices and one verbal warning and were caught by an avalanche. It is an unhappy fact that people who have skied for a lifetime can be caught out, in part because they have the skill and snowcraft to be able to leave the crowded pistes. One mis-

Skiers at Samedan in the Engadine observe the path of an avalanche. There are three main types of avalanche – powder, wet snow and wind slab. This was a powderslide.

judgement, however, can have gruesome consequences. All who leave the piste should do so either with a guide or, if they are confident of their own abilities or knowledge of an area, with a minimum of safety and rescue equipment. What flies without wings, strikes without hand and sees without eyes? The avalanche beast! It is an animal of legend among mountain people. Plenty have felt its fangs – more than 20 people a year are killed in the Alps.

On 16 March 1958, a German doctor, Marcel Kurz, and his wife, decided to spend their last day after a medical congress at Davos on the Parsenn. Two skiers had been killed in the area in the previous two days. Signs on the Weissfluhjoch told people to stay on marked runs, but partway down the pair branched off into the Meierhof gully. There was no track in the deep snow, which was becoming heavier with a brilliant sun beating down on the overnight snowfall. Just near the exit of the gully, it became so sticky that the couple stopped to wax their skis. It was a beautiful day, and they were in no hurry. Suddenly, above them, two skiers appeared. A few seconds later there was a snapping noise and as a shout, 'Achtung, Lawine!' rang out from the strangers, the slope opposite them began to slip. Kurz and his wife tried desperately to run, but it was hopeless. The snow hissed over them and they were enveloped.

Kurz's first thought was the irony that all had happened within minutes of his last skiing of the season. He was angry, and worried for his children, but curiously unafraid. Frau Kurz wondered how far away her husband was, and then remembered the Parsenn rescue service and thought what help they would be mounting. Both lost consciousness in about three minutes. One of the skiers who had shouted the warning looked at his watch. It was 11.50. Quickly they made for the snow heap, marked the point where they had last seen the victims, and one skied off for

Below and Right:
Powder trails in the Spanish Pyrenées and the Canadian Monashees.
Snow has countless forms, varying according to time of season, day, location, depth, age and variety of layering.
Consistent powder snow is one of the great joys — when you can find it.

help while the other kept searching, prodding with inverted ski stick. At 12.02 the klaxons sounded in the Parsenndienst headquarters and the rescue attempt began. Avalanche dogs, doctors and rescue teams with sleds were pulled together. Melchior Schild, of the Swiss Institute of Snow and Avalanche Research, and an expert on avalanche dogs, abandoned his Sunday lunch and set off with his Alsatian dog, Iso. To save time, he motored to the bottom of the gully and clambered up the $2\frac{1}{2}$ miles of deep snow to the accident site. They were there in 20 minutes. Iso, howling with excitement, set to work at once. After three minutes he stopped and began to scratch. Schild noted the spot and sent the dog off again. Five minutes later, and a little farther to the right, Iso began to dig frantically. Schild called the dog to him, then sent him off to the first spot. The dog scratched again, this time much more urgently. Schild dug away at the spot. Presently he found a man's shoulders, three feet down. In the other place he found a boot and ankle, four feet deep. At 13.40, one hour and 50 minutes after the avalanche, Dr and Frau Kurz were lifted clear, both

purple in the face. Kurz was half conscious, and under oxygen and heart stimulation he slowly regained strength. Frau Kurz was in a worse state. Her jaw was clamped shut so firmly it was impossible to pass the suction pump tube into her mouth. A medical helper smashed off an eye tooth with a pocket knife handle and the tube was inserted. Her life was saved, but not without a struggle still. On the way to hospital she twice needed artificial respiration. They were lucky, both of them, that four doctors who had been attending the conference were immediately at hand. Four days after the avalanche they drove back home to Stuttgart. Dr Kurz suffered no reaction until four days afterwards he was shown colour transparencies of the two holes from which he and his wife were saved. Someone had used his camera to take the shot. Dr Kurz was so overcome he had to lie down. Both believed their faith in the rescue service played an extraordinary part in their survival, but the skiers who saw the accident acted correctly and quickly. The Kurzes also thanked the sheer chance that they had removed their anoraks and pullovers in the warm

Sparkling new snow, a wide, smiling sky, and soaring, swooping through the powder. It's the nearest man or woman gets to flying, the champagne of ski life. Skiers love it East and West – on Mount Daietsu, in Japan; on Aspen Mountain, Colorado.

sunshine, allowing their bodies to cool more rapidly and reducing oxygen needs.

This, of course, is the horrific face of snow, albeit with a smile to finish with. Scientifically it has been elusive. Snow crystal research is of recent origin. Wilson Bentley photographed 6,000 different forms of crystal, but barely disturbed the surface. The forms are myriad, but they start from a basic hexagonal. It is formed in the atmosphere when air containing water vapour rises and cools and condenses on to the tiny particles always in the atmosphere. Below freezing point the ice particles grow as more water vapour attaches. In this process, known as sublimation, the substance is changing from a gaseous to a solid state, or vice versa, without passing through its normal liquid state. So, water vapour is changing

straight to ice, the particles get heavier and heavier, and finally fall in the form of snow crystals. Stars, rods, spikes, plates, needles are formed, with infinite variations. Temperature and humidity much affect the sublimation process, so crystals passing through cloud and blown by wind suffer different influences. A crystal falling at high altitude generally is much different to one falling lower down. Up top it will be small, down below a larger, dendritic (star- or branch-shaped) flake. Crystals forming round salt particles as opposed to dust will have very different characteristics. Thus Scottish or Hokkaido snow, falling close to seaboards, greatly varies from Colorado snow, with the sea a thousand miles away and more. In higher temperatures, flakes can be huge. Hail of the sort which may pierce a normal anorak like grapeshot on the Cairngorms of Scotland has invariably passed through thick fog or cloud, the cold water freezing on to the crystal and creating a kind of pellet.

Change goes on and on. As the crystal or flake reaches the ground there is a process known as snow metamorphosis. Within a few days, two feet of

snow may be down to a foot. New snow contains around 90 per cent of trapped air. This gradually seeps away, and the snow crystal itself changes its nature. The fine points of the stars or branches of the dendritic crystal disappear, and the crystal starts to integrate with others. Almost everyone has delighted in the squeak of boots trampling new snow. It is, literally, the noise of crystals being crunched up, and does not occur once the snow has started to metamorphose.

Two other forms of metamorphosis are more understandable in their effect than their scientific form. Constructive metamorphosis is the effect of water rising from warmer crystals in the lower layers and freezing on to crystals higher up in the form of a hexagonal cup. These cup crystals may provide an extremely unstable layer in the snow cover. Finally there is 'melt' metamorphosis, which is the growth of ice granules by constant thawing and refreezing. Skiers ought to know of one other type of crystal, the surface hoar, because it too can represent danger. On calm, clear nights, especially after a succession of them, water vapour sublimes on to snow crystals, leaving glistening leaf-like

plates on the surface. The sun quickly melts them during the day, but not on shaded north slopes. A heavy snowfall on these can create an avalanche slope. They are fragile crystals which will break when the load gets too great.

So, surface snow conditions will vary according to time of season, day, location on the mountain, depth, age and variety of layering. Every few yards will have a different character to which the skier, first with his eye if he is sufficiently experienced, otherwise by the feel of the snow under his skis, must react. A skier will have this 'feel' to a remarkable degree. Jean-Claude Killy once remarked, 'To be a great skier you must have intelligence of the feet.' Franz Klammer, the Austrian Olympic downhill champion, was once 'wired to

the snow' with his skis electronically recording contact. It showed without question that his ski soles had better contact than any other Austrian ski team member of that time. Beginners as well as experts ought to have some knowledge of the different kinds of snow they will ski on. In late December, January and early February it will mostly be cold, well-beaten snow. Tractors may be out all night after a new fall to provide a beaten piste in the morning. Otherwise they turn and air older snow to prevent the formation of hard-pack motorways. But Ratracs cannot be everywhere, or may be restricted by fog or cloud after a recent fall. In those circumstances the skier will meet powder conditions. The further from the sea he is, the drier the powder will be,

and the easier it is to ski in. The powder hounds of the Rocky Mountain states go to almost any lengths — by plane, helicopter, snomobile — to find it. Alpine powder is rarer, and shorter lived, and at its best when about a foot of it has fallen on a firm snow base. Sparkling new snow, a wide, smiling sky, and soaring, swooping through the powder. It's the nearest man or woman gets to

Trail preparation requires expert knowledge of snow characteristics. Snow tractors tow ridged rollers to compress new snow, leaving air pockets. The hard-packed snow helps trail conservation making it less sensitive to temperature change. Tractors may also tow scrapers to level moguls, the bumps formed by skiers' repeated passage.

flying, the champagne of ski life. Like all good things, it does not last. If the snow stops it quickly becomes tamped down. If it continues it becomes deep and heavy to turn in, indeed the most dangerous conditions for inexperienced or novice skiers.

Later in the season, in late February, March or April, the novice will meet corn, or spring snow, with the warm sun causing granulation just before and after midday. Before it gets too mushy or refreezes, spring snow provides a wonderfully easy surface for turning. The skis swish rather than hiss through it; there are not the fine showers of powder snow spray whipped up by his ski tails; but the skier's tension automatically eases and he finds it is not such a difficult sport after all.

It is more likely that each day and each run will pose different conditions and challenges. You may think you know a run blindfold. Along comes a better skier who leads you down a more direct route, faster than you have been before, and everything is changed. In good conditions, bottlenecks will develop icy, rocky patches. Sheet ice is the most difficult of all surfaces, for expert and beginner alike. On the day after the 1978 World Downhill Championship at Garmisch-Partenkirchen, I found myself, by mistake, having misread a sign, on the famous ice wall of the course. The previous day, downhill aces like Walcher, Veith, Grissman, Klammer and Plank were taking it straight at 80 mph. In a sense, it was the easy way. To try and traverse was impossible. The ice

glinted bleak and black across the full breadth of the hill, with fencing uncompromisingly penning you to the hill. A young German soldier tore by, glimpsed the slope falling away in front of him, put in one check, then another, caught an edge, and somersaulted 100 metres to the bottom before skidding wildly into the palings. He did not move for about half a minute, then slowly picked

Summer glacier skiing is growing in popularity. The ice bedrock provides a smooth surface as encouraging to novices as to racers training for a hard winter season.

himself up. Mercifully he was unhurt. My Canadian broadcaster companion suddenly yelled, 'Watch out.' Behind us, another soldier was hurtling over the hill crest – upside down. He turned turtle three times before thudding into the fencing. Again there was an awful pause. Again the skier slowly rose, unhurt. My Canadian friend yelled his instruction: 'Bounce real hard. Keep those edges hot.' It worked. Usually a skier will avoid glare ice by picking his path. Nearly always it has patches of churned ice giving the ski edges a better grip. Sometimes it is unavoidable and the only answer, easier to postulate than accomplish, is to relax. Tensing up almost certainly means a tumble. Few enjoy sheet ice. The only exceptions I have met are the Canadian downhill racers such as Ken Read and Dave Irwin, who grew up with glare ice at Canadian latitudes, and know some of their European rivals can be psyched out by it. Hard icy conditions should remind everyone to check their ski edges. Hire shops may not like skis returned for sharpening. Filing wears them out that much quicker. For the holiday skier on hard-packed pistes it can make all the difference between semi-controlled slither and a calm, enjoyable run.

The two other types of snow to bother about are crust, which is what it sounds, a frosted surface layer, and decayed snow known variously as porridge, mashed potato or crud. Crust is encountered by early risers on a main run. It is the hoar frosted snow I described earlier in the chapter. Thick or variable crust presents problems. Skiing in it has a curious stop-go sensation. Straight running is not difficult but it requires a sophisticated technique and a degree of fitness to ski it for any distance. Holiday skiers, in general, can tackle thin crust if they don't require to turn much. Otherwise they should avoid it. Porridge, mashed potato, crud . . . it is all onomatopoeia for taking off your skis and going home. It is snow in an advanced state of decay, usually at a low-lying resort towards the end of the season.

Skiers within a car ride of mountains soon learn to study the weather maps and forecasts and make objective decisions. You rarely ski enjoyably in bad snow. If you are hooked to a fixed week or fortnight and a package deal you make the best of it, but confidence is more likely to be sapped than helped. The need to choose carefully when making a long-range holiday decision cannot be stressed too much. Love of skiing should never be a blind love.

1

What to do in an avalanche:

If the break occurs under your feet, try to leap upwards or sideways to snow which may not be avalanching.

* Try to delay being carried down as long as possible, jabbing ski poles in the snow as brakes.

* Try to get rid of your skis and poles as rapidly as possible. The additional leverage they impose on limbs increases the risk of twists and fractures.

* If under way, keep the mouth shut and make strong swimming motions with arms and legs to stay on the surface.

* As the avalanche slows, try to create space with the hands in front of the nose and mouth. A few inches of breathing space could be valuable.

* Once stopped, make one determined effort to escape upwards. Test for upward direction by spitting and watching or feeling the saliva drip downwards.

* Fear may put breathing up from 15 to more than 35 breaths per minute. Since you cannot fight or run away, try to keep calm. Shout if you hear helpers close, but sound does not carry far in snow.

1
This powder slope at Verbier, Switzerland looks innocent enough. And most inviting for the powder hound.

2
Not so innocent after all. The true danger of the slope is seen as the skier breaks the delicate adhesion of the layers of snow. The top layer cracks and splits and starts to slide.

3
The break widens, more snow slides, carrying the skier down with it.

4
More snow is collected, gathering momentum as it goes. Miraculously, the skier is left behind. He could easily have been borne hundreds of feet further down and buried.

5
By incredible luck, the skier is uninjured. After this slide, he will be more wary.

2

3

4

5

Vacations and Snow

Today, society's best brainwash

The simplest answer to why millions living far from mountains now want to ski is the oblong eye in the corner — television. Where families and friends passed on the good news by word of mouth from the Thirties to the Fifties, from the Sixties onwards people could see for themselves what a good thing it could be. Simultaneously came the package tour explosion which catered for the demand with profit margins shaved closer for the turnover snow holidays could attract. Longer holidays, more leisure, increased concern and instruction for sport and recreation. It all came together.

A ski package simply rolls together all or most of the elements of travel, hotel, transfers, equipment hire, lessons, lift passes, insurance, airport fees and other incidentals on one sum payable in instalments before you go. The insurance will even look after the possibility of illness if you cannot go, as well as the

These telecabines, or gondolas, at Verbier, Switzerland, are among the many forms of uphill transport.

possibility of doing yourself a thousand pounds worth of damage, or someone claiming a couple of hundred thousand dollars from you if you smash into him on the ski slope. Discounts vary according to the season of the year. Christmas and New Year are high, so are mid-February to mid-March and the Easter period. Discounts are biggest in January when the snow is often at its best, and the lift queue shortest, but the discos will not be packed except at weekends, when locals also make for the slopes, and the ski day will end at 4 p.m.

The perfect resort? A *New York Daily News* writer, enthusing over her grand-sized pisco sour about Portillo, Chile, also warned of O'Higgins' revenge, also known as Chile-itis, a bowel infection which can pinion skiers to their bathrooms for 24 hours. She advised a pre-ski course of yoghourt, which sounds better than pre-ski exercises.

Small World, an English travel operator, had a go as follows: 'The perfect resort has extensive slopes facing in all directions (needed by skiers who tend to face in all directions when skiing); a profusion of uphill transport, preferably in closed gondolas and cable cars for cold weather, and drag lifts and chair lifts for sunny days; no traffic in

the village, but an efficient minibus service linking village centre, main hotels, the lift terminals and neighbouring resorts; a choice of live bands and discos, all busy but not overcrowded, with no entrance fees and with drinks at bar prices; plenty of mountain restaurants with instant service at lunchtime; ski instructors devoted to ski instruction by day and après-ski instruction by night (presumably for the ladies); ski slopes high enough to guarantee snow all season but low enough not to get too cold in December, and accessible in all weathers; an attractive olde worlde alpine village but no walking between hotels, chalets and lifts; and, above all, low prices for everything.'

Small World goes on, perhaps not surprisingly, to point out that no such Ski Utopialp exists. A purpose-built resort with every lift emanating from the interior of its vast single building complex can never be a traditional picturesque village; a lift system which can cope with the morning rush hour will have a high-priced ski pass because its system is basically under utilised; lively night life is dependent upon sufficient custom to justify its existence and may therefore mean a well-frequented resort and consequently some rush-hour waiting for lifts and for restaurant service on the slopes. And, of course, if it really is Goodalp, as opposed to Badalp, with more than a single cable car to get you up from the valley to a 'circus' of runs, will it have snow when you get there? Advance booking cannot guarantee that.

Europe and the USA have highly geared snow industries which seek to meet halfway the vacationer who seriously plans his holiday. The USA in general is more aware of beginner worries and ignorances than Europe. Americans at Alpine resorts persist with their questions and don't readily take no for an answer. Their resorts, indeed much of their lifestyle, are geared to consumer needs. American hire equip-

Left:
Slopes above Tignes, in France, link with those of Val d'Isère to form one of the largest ski areas in the world.

Right above:
There's more to a ski holiday than just skiing, for example, a sleigh ride like this in the Italian Dolomites.

Right:
Rush-hour in a cable-car is as bad as a rush-hour in a big city. This cable-car takes you up high above St. Moritz.

ment is usually of a very high standard and up to date. The same can be said of parts of France and West Germany, but not everywhere else. Television shows skiing at its peak – World Cup and Olympic races with Stenmark, the Mahres and Klammer, freestyle with Genia Fuller and John Eaves. The bug bites. People become obsessed with the thoughts of soaring like birds on sunlit uplands. They yearn for romance and enjoyment, for large, fun-loving groups. Then the bug nips a trifle. Skiing is hard. Skiing is tough. The sun does not always shine. The boots hurt. You can break an ankle in the streets easier than you can on the slopes. The instructor's breath smells of garlic. You run out of French and German phrases. Too much ski love gets nipped in the bud. The drop-out rate has been put at two in three. Yet still the jets from London and New York spill out skiers by the thousand at Geneva, Milan, Munich, Zurich, Denver and Montreal. For every man or woman

who falls there are two to take the place.

Tour operators are getting the message. Love need not be blind. The couple turning up in London to buy a holiday are likely to have a calculator at hand. Skiing is expensive, fashionable, voguish. But people like to choose for themselves how and where to economise – if they want to economise. They want to be presented with options, and if do-it-yourself has advantages, they want to know some of that too. Condominium, flatlet or chalet living has boomed among people wanting independence from hotel menus and timetables. Motoring into the mountains has also multiplied – although he is a foolish driver who does not stow chains, if he is not already on snow tyres, a shovel, tow cable, warning sign and sack of sand in the boot. In Austria, a first aid kit is compulsory and, in any case, should be included when driving could be hazardous.

More people are buying rather than

Enjoying yourself; that's what skiing is all about.

Inset:
Zermatt, with the famous Matterhorn, is one of the most beautiful ski areas in the world. But not the cheapest.

Below:
You can get a healthy, mid-winter tan in the high mountains, but a barrier cream is essential.

hiring equipment before they reach the snow centres. Ski retailers in London or New York must offer expertise with their sales patter. Tour operators must know which resorts have satellites sharing lift pass arrangements. That St. Christoph, Stuben, Zürs and Lech share the wonderful snowfields of the Arlberg with St. Anton. That Söll, Worgl, Westendorf, Kirchberg, St. Johann, Jochberg and Fieberbrunn are all around Kitzbühel – and a bit cheaper, too. They want to know which French resorts other than Les Arcs teach Ski Evolutif, and which Italian lift company is working with his neighbour. There is nothing worse than being on the same mountain as two lift groups at war with each other. Italy, with its relative cheapness, still has not solved this problem in a number of resorts. Which places are best for beginners, which for intermediates, which for experts – the operator is expected to know and pass objective judgement. To offer more help, specialist ski magazines are available in all Western countries.

Operators can often book ski school at a discount, and for all grades up to advanced this is usually advised. For intermediates it is a way of getting to know people as well as to improve technique, for beginners it is essential. Advanced skiers may want to observe the quality of the instruction and the waiting phases before they commit themselves. If tows are crowded on popular runs they are probably better off with a companion getting in some mileage elsewhere. Private lessons are always possible for topping up or ironing out faults. Local knowledge may then be helpful in finding uncluttered runs and fresh snow.

Cross-country vacations are still a novelty to most Americans and British, but they are catching on. The choice of places grows steadily, and there are not the physical limitations as there are with Alpine ski. Inn to inn through the Green Mountains of Vermont is becoming an attractive proposition for reasonably fit people who have not skied much before; a holiday boom is starting.

The Austrian Alps are renowned for their scenic beauty. The Lentaschtal in the Tyrol is also a good area for cross-country enthusiasts.

Right:
Falling is all part of the fun, sometimes.

Below:
And after your falls, soak away the aches and pains in a heated pool, like this one in Italy.

Equipment

The technical, the practical, the fashionable skiing has it all

As he skids off the ski lift and stands at the top of the slope preparing for his first run down of the day, the modern skier will be sporting equipment and clothes worth at least as much as the holiday itself if he is packaged from one of the North European countries to the Alps.

A Swiss bank estimated in the late 1970s that the world's 35 million skiers supported an industry with a total turnover of 16 billion dollars, including travel, hotels, equipment, clothing and other ancillaries. They spend two billion dollars annually on skis, boots, clothing, sun glasses, cosmetics and other bits. Judged by an American research report commissioned by the magazine *Skiing*, the Swiss estimate of world skiers is much too conservative; *Skiing* estimated the US Alpine figure alone at 14 million and cross-country well over two million, and the figures swell every year. Incontrovertibly, it represents a huge market,

A Swiss bank estimated that the world's 35 million skiers supported an industry with a total turnover of 16 billion dollars in the late 1970s – and growing annually. Over two billion dollars are spent on skis alone.

and every customer a major investment.

The ski industry proudly claims that there are now no bad skis, only different skis at different prices to accommodate a range of weight, ability and attitude. It is pointless a middle-aged man of over 14 stone who skis only a fortnight a year paying a huge sum for skis better suited to an Austrian downhill star. He might want a firmer ski than a 16-year-old girl to allow for his weight. He will also want a ski made shorter and softer for easy turning and handling. If he is cautious, intermediate and slow, he will hardly be concerned with the short ski reinforced towards the tip for straight running at higher speeds. If he is fairly aggressive, reasonably fit and a quickish learner he might be advised to go for just that. If he wants to go off-piste into soft snow that is another scene. Softer, longer skis are then advisable.

But there's the rub. Who offers the advice? Which voice to believe in the hubbub of claim and counter-claim? Few manufacturers can resist a bit of technical blarney to convince the would-be buyer that his ski has more than the rest. In a complex world of shorts, compacts, mids, standards, long, soft, competition, freestyle, ballet, bump and super everything, who or what to believe? Is it necessary to have a grasp of sidecut, flex pattern, side deflection, damping and torsional rigidity? The answer for the fortnight-a-year skier must be qualified. There are a few essentials he or she should try and grasp. The rest is for the technically minded, who have a natural or educated grasp of what goes on under the bonnet, for the people who live in snow and must learn to differentiate by fine margins, and for the advanced to expert skier. No two pairs of skis seem to be alike in the lift queue, but a great deal of this is badge engineering or colour

Skis now come in three main types. The majority of holiday skiers are on Compacts. The introduction has revolutionised modern teaching techniques.

cosmetics. It is true – there are few bad skis these days, only badly maintained skis, or wrong skis for a particular performer or snow surface. Price is not necessarily the best guide, it is what the maker can get for the skis. Skis are best defined in three main styles – Compact, Mid-length and Standard. A *Compact* is a ski designed to be used in a length below your own head height – which may be anything between 150 and 190 centimetres. The main characteristics are little waisting, the almost uniform-width ski giving greater stability in straight, downhill running. Normal, waisted skis at this length do not give the necessary stability. When they originally hit the market, Compacts were 80 mm wide. Now they are 70 mm. It doesn't sound a lot, but the difference is 15 per cent of the sole of the ski. The only skis still made in the super wide widths are the very short skis of GLM or Ski Evolutif (See Ski School).

A well-built man will best use a Compact of 170 to 180 centimetres, a lightweight girl 150 centimetres. An average Compact length is 160. Compacts represent about 80 per cent of the English speaking market. Their great contribution has been to get people

skiing better much sooner. The more people ski, the better they ski. Fortnight-a-year people on Compacts get in more of the mileage they desperately need – and become better skiers as a result. Skiing standards in Europe and North America have bounded ahead since they were introduced.

Mid-length, or cruising, skis are a stepping stone to the standard ski or the ultimate for better, weekend or recreational skiers. They are waisted skis of 185 cm to 205 cm which will carve a turn more easily and precisely. You turn on a Compact by sliding or skidding on to a new course. The better skier, with superior edge control, can use the reverse cambering into the snow of his waisted ski to make a precise turn. Most modern mid-lengths have softish tips to make turning in bumps, or moguls, as they are often known, more easy. Only in the middle to late 1970s did ski construction become so sophisticated that all major manufacturers could produce an article that was both flexible and strong. This was the great leap forward.

A huge range of high-quality, mid-length skis are on the market. The good ski is the one you grow used to, rather

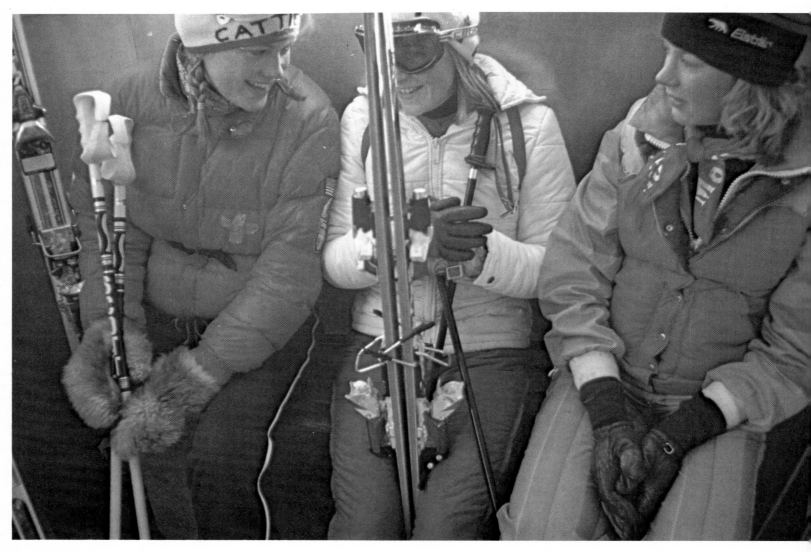

Comfortable boots are the most important item of skiing equipment. Ill-fitting boots are probably responsible for more dropouts from the sport than anything else.

like the car in your garage. You get to know its limits – and yours. And you keep the rev counter out of the red, even after a lunchtime schnapps.

Weight is more of a guideline to the best ski length than height. You have to be honest with yourself and the scales. If you are heavily built you add ten centimetres. If you are light you take off ten. The time to go on to a mid-length is when you can manage a parallel turn in reasonable snow conditions. If you go into it too early you are likely to hold up your progress into becoming a good parallel skier. If height is used as a criterion, it is 10 to 15 centimetres above the head.

Standard Skis are around 185 cm for a woman or particularly light man to 205 cm, the more usual length. They should be anything from 15 to 20 cm above the head. They are for good parallel skiers able to schuss at speeds over 30 mph (the average intermediate is more often under 15 mph). Skis for recreational speed are a little softer in flex and torsion (twisting capability) than racing skis, but give a stable ride at relatively high speeds. Modern Standards have more torsion throughout their length than the skis of the Sixties and early Seventies, and are easier to handle in soft snow and bumps. They cost somewhat more, and after two or three seasons have virtually no second-hand value. Skiers good enough for these don't want second best. Compact owners may get back half their purchase price after an equivalent number of seasons.

Love of skiing is sometimes a good tumble in the snow, picking yourself up, dusting yourself down, and starting all over again. It means you have made your mistake, tried to correct, maybe overcompensated and, anyway, finished tail up or down in the snow. Everyone laughs – quietly, or right out loud. Falling because of stepping on a banana skin, or a patch of ice or snow, is an elemental form of humour. Who doesn't like to see a pompous person deflated? You may not be pompous, but for the ski class you'll pass for the major or the clergyman when you land on your backside. Funnily enough, you'll probably laugh too. If you haven't seen a couple of Austrian or Swiss ten year olds dive head first down a powder snow slope, bowling over and over like playful kittens, then you've missed one of the joys of the snow scene. There's a bit of that in a grown-up ski tumble. You actually enjoy it. Unless, of course, your skis don't come off, and the leverage of several feet of ski on a 150 to 180 lb human body strikes just above the boot top, and there you are, lying in the snow, not laughing and joking, but with a spiral fracture of your tibia, or a shattered knee.

Which is where a vital component comes in – ski bindings. For people new to skiing a binding needs explanation. It has apparently contradictory meanings. Its first function is to hold you on to your ski amid the variety of physical shocks it gets on the simplest of nursery slopes. The pressures of a downhill racer's ski as he corrects violently or hits a bump or hollow at 80 mph are infinitely greater. The bindings must be variously adjustable to accept these shocks, but release when they assume intolerable forces for the leg bones under pressure. Like everything else in skiing, they have become even more sophisticated in recent times, and certainly far removed from the primitive osiers of Sondre Norheim. The balance between retention and release must be exact or a cry of joy suddenly becomes a cry of anguish.

The cheapest binding is about half the cost of the cheapest ski, the most expensive rather more. Cheaper bindings these days are perfectly safe for the slower skier. It is the fast, expert skier who requires the sophistications of the more expensive article. But any binding, it must be stressed, is only as good as the precision and care with which it is adjusted and maintained. The simplest binding has a range of settings, and if you haven't bought them new to be able to read carefully the instructions, you must never be afraid to check with a hire shop or a ski school instructor if you have any doubt that they are not set to your abilities. An inexperienced skier does better to err on the lower side of the setting. It is dangerous to lose a ski without good reason at high speed. At low speeds it rarely does much harm. Not to lose a ski at slow speeds is a greater danger. Some people do themselves damage without moving. Waiting in a queue, standing and chatting, they turn or twist, lose balance, and fall over without acquiring the forces needed to release the binding. Fortunately, the dangers of this are being reduced as more bindings are introduced with releases at a greater variety of angles.

There are two main types of binding, working to different principles. *Heel and*

toe bindings are designed for you to slide your toe welts under the flange of the front piece, and click down with your heel on a rear piece, which firmly holds your foot on the ski. Most have three angles of release, upwards at the heel, and to left and right at the toe. More sophisticated designs allow upward movement at the toe. Friction can hinder release, but all heel and toe designs have a pad, usually teflon, underneath the ball of the foot to assist sideways release. A modern binding has built-in elasticity which allows small, momentary movement of the boot at higher speeds, returning it to centre. When the twisting forces become sustained, the binding releases.

Plate bindings were introduced in the Seventies by Ernst Gertsch, a pioneer Alpine skier from Wengen. They rapidly acquired popularity originally among novice and intermediate skiers, but also, as design became more sophisticated, expert skiers too. They work on an entirely different principle, with the boot attached to a plate which comes away with the boot in the event of a fall. Since the plate and not the boot is in contact with the ski and release mech-

anisms, the friction problem virtually disappears. A greater variety of release angles have now been introduced into modern plate bindings. Beginners, who are more likely to come out of their skis, find them easier when remounting, and do not have problems cleaning the snow off their boots before clipping back, as may be the case with heel and toe bindings.

Many bindings now come with a built-in ski stopper. This is a sprung clip under the boot sole which automatically releases a horseshoe shaped prong when the skier comes out of his bindings. The prongs dig into the snow and prevent a ski sliding away, gathering momentum, and either leaving a skier to scramble down the mountain

Above:
A standard step-in ski binding. The retractable ski-stopper can be seen at the heel. The boot has a polyurethane shell, with a padded inner boot lined with leather.

Middle:
A plate binding. The boot is attached to a plate which detaches from the ski in a fall.

Right:
A mountain-touring binding. The heel is allowed to lift for easier walking but can be clipped down for downhill skiing.

Left:
Falling can be part of the fun. But well-adjusted bindings are essential for release at the right moment. Note how the skier's left foot has been released by his binding because of his fall.

carrying one ski – not so easy, and indeed dangerous, in a blizzard with snow up to the thighs – or hurtle down the mountain to smash into some unsuspecting skier below. Otherwise, bindings have a safety strap attachment which the skier clips round his ankle to retain the ski if he releases involuntarily. In a higher speed fall there is a danger of the ski windmilling on the end of the strap and clipping the skier painfully. The one disadvantage to the pronged stopper is the possibility of the skier plummeting on, leaving his 'stopped' ski buried in soft snow. Reclamation can be a long and tedious business. Many people prefer to take this risk rather than suffer the inconvenience of the strap, which nearly always must be unclipped after a fall, with the risk of the ski running away on a steeper slope, and all the bending and stretching of reclipping.

Poles, batons, sticks, as they are variously called, are not the most loved part of most people's equipment. They do not have the grace and apparent craftsmanship of the ski, nor the obvious function of the boot. But where and how a skier plants them will make a great difference to the beginner in his first tentative motions, and to the expert when he makes his turns. These, too, have come a long way since the Arlberg pioneer planted his single clothes line pole and stick rod, so to speak. Modern designs are much influenced by the German DIN standards, which demand that they are as safe as possible, both whilst skiing and when being brandished in crowded places. Handles have been introduced with a so-called sword grip, a shaped plastic guard which grips the gloved hand over the knuckles, but is articulated so that the hand slips out readily in a fall. Other designs, retaining the leather or plastic strap, have a plug-in arrangement so the strap comes away with the hand. Tips may no longer be sheer points under DIN standards, and are serrated to reduce impact damage. On the snow the tip still digs in up to the basket, two to three inches above. Basket designs vary: the type with circular looped patterns may catch in boot clips, and heavy-duty plastic flutes are preferred by many. Ski poles are made with a high centre of gravity and should feel almost wand-like. It is better that they are slightly too short than too long. Ideally they are 30 to 35 centimetres (10 to 12 inches) below the armpit with the point on a hard floor.

Boots are the most important item of skiing equipment. Ill-fitting boots are probably responsible for more drop-outs from the sport than anything else. A ski boot ought to be loved as a ski is loved. A goodish ski can be acquired almost anywhere. A boot is a totally personal thing. Once worn in, it is all but irreplaceable until it wears out, or is superseded by a superior design. Ten years after winning his three gold medals at Grenoble, Jean-Claude Killy still possessed the leather boots he wore. 'Once in a while I put them on,' he said once. 'They were really fantastic, because that leather was like underwear. It was so close to the skin you were able to use a hundred per cent of the boot.'

The English seemed to cling on longest to leather boots; but then, you can still see some with the coiled wire and clip Kandahar bindings of the Thirties and Forties. Equipment you know and care for has a worth apart from its function. Leather boots, Kandahar bindings and laminated wood skis went together. Leather boots and modern bindings do not. A modern heel binding may require ten stone of force for a release. That isn't much for a boot with a rigid thermoplastic or polyure-thane shell. A leather boot, perhaps well worn, with a great deal of forward give, may permit a great deal of 'give' in a slow, forward fall. So, the necessary amount of pressure for release may not be forthcoming. The result: a possible fracture, torn Achilles' tendon, or muscular or ligament pulls.

The modern boot has an outer shell most likely made of the two man-made substances I have mentioned, and a padded, usually detachable, inner. The cheaper variety of plastic will be more flexible but less durable. The more expensive boots, in the harder plastics, will provide more support and last longer. They are likely to incorporate design characteristics for the faster, better skier, for example more forward lean and height. Some boots are articulated and clipped for varying forward rake. Increasingly designers have tried to reduce the number of clips employed. Hanson of America has pioneered the rear entry boot and interesting concepts whereby the boot adjusts to the foot, not vice versa.

Most inner linings are detachable so that they can be removed for drying. Cheaper linings are preformed. Most

are bladders filled with putty-like substance which moulds to the shape of the foot, which itself changes shape slightly as the blood flow increases with increased effort. Most boots come now with standard sole patterns, as much to avoid falling in icy village streets when walking as to ensure proper adjustment to bindings. Streets can be more dangerous than ski slopes. Boot buying is one of the most anxious chores a skier can have. In a shop he rarely feels anything but clumping and awkward. The rear-entry boot is progressing towards a better balance between skiing practicability, lightness and comfort, but true love with the ski boot remains a blessed but rare happening.

It is a curious skier who stands at the top of the run accoutred only in his skis, bindings, boots and batons. The skier is likely to have paid as much again for the clothes he/she is wearing – ski suit, or dungarees (salopettes) and anorak, down vest, sweater, cotton roll neck and underclothes, thick socks, leather/plastic gloves with warm linings, and ski hat. At one time most of the cash went into après-ski clothes, while on the slopes many men, certainly many

These German grass-skis run on the same caterpillar principle as tanks. But grass tends to be harder to fall on than snow.

This Swedish all-in-one suit is ideal. It is practical, warm, comfortable and stylish.

Englishmen, were in something like their garden clothes. In those days skiing had more social cachet than fashion on the slopes. Men wore baggy pants, ladies went from ankle-length dresses to equally baggy pants, and kept their silk evening trousers, lamé jumpers and gold boots for the evening.

In the 1960s came the skiwear revolution along with the rest of the Swinging Scene, and the pace hardly slowed in the Seventies, although fashions switched and swayed. Lange advertised their ski girl with the boobs and it didn't raise a Brrr!

Space-age racers emerged in the ultimate figure-hugging shiny plastic sheath suits, cutting split seconds off their downhill times, but became human cannon balls when they fell. Not just that, they climbed out drenched in perspiration, wringing out their underclothes in their bath tubs. The fashion trade wet look posed equal dangers for less able skiers, who fell more often if not as fast. The racers rebelled; the FIS clamped down on the sheath suits. The wet look hung on, but with a cultivated roughness to prevent excessive slide after a fall.

Fashion, though, stays king for many. An expensive item may not be the best designed for the job, only the best looking. Lined and quilted one-piece outers are obviously best for a mountainside at ten under zero. The wise look for adjustability in their clothing. At breakfast the sun may be shining and the mountain glinting like a travel brochure picture. But mountain weather changes fast. Freezing fog or blinding snow may fall like a curtain straight after the mountain cafeteria lunch. No-one notices a fashion plate in conditions like those. North American experience of extreme cold in northerly latitudes has brought more appropriate clothes to skiing than jeans. The puffy-look duvet and gilet, vests and jackets for really cold weather, are examples. Swedish freestyle teams introduced some way-out, though practical, designs. The Scots clung on to the cagoul to combat wet cold. Figure-hugging fashion is not always strong on pockets. But skiers need places to put things – sun or snow glasses, goggles, money, lift passes, lip seals and sun creams. Skiing is casual and easy-going, but not all the time in every place. It can be hard, difficult, even cruel. Fashion people may enjoy parading round the resorts, but they must enjoy the tough stuff too.

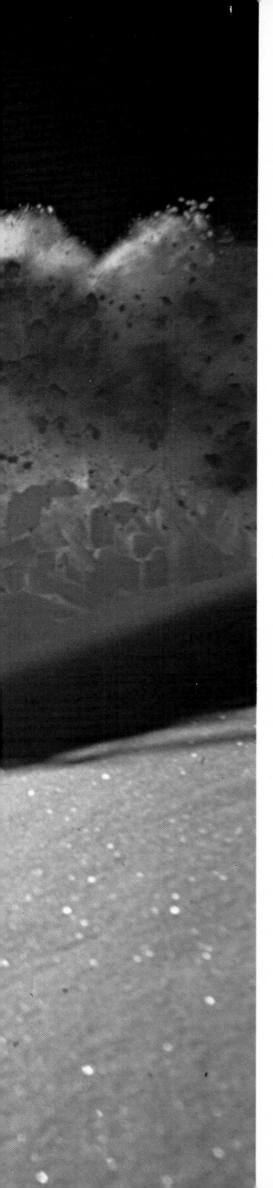

Ski School

At all levels, the challenge of the mental and physical processes

Skiing is a true love of millions. Naturally it does not always run smoothly. In the high temples of skiing, the learning schools of Austria, France, Switzerland and America, the altercations and controversies are endless. This was so in the beginning, with strong Scandinavian objections to the recognition of Alpine skiing, and will surely continue to the end.

No aspect of skiing has been more controversial than the Learning Game. Skiing does not come gift packaged. For many it is a compulsive but expensive fortnight in a mountain wonderland, with their mental and physical prowess challenged every inch of the way. Each country dependent on the ski holidaymaker for an important part of its tourist trade spends small fortunes on creating an individual image. Thus the New Austrian System, the New French way, GLM and Ski Evolutif may sometimes seem part of the whole Madison Avenue

The flying, floating exuberance of deep powder is skiing's greatest experience.

selling apparatus. To see it wholly as this is too cynical. The getaway holidaymaker from crowded, noisy cities does need help to cope with his mountain environment. The learning systems are created for him, not the young Alpine bergler, native of one of the mountain valleys, who grows up in snow.

At the same time, as Arnold Lunn perceived long ago, no country with a rich tourist industry can afford to see its young racers outclassed by another country. This only suggests that their techniques lack something, and that their ski schools are inadequate. Huge resources are, therefore, poured into national racing teams, partly from the industry, partly from the state, and the major countries vie to hold Winter Olympic Games and World Championships which familiarise their national identity and resorts, and, hopefully, provide gold medals for their racers. The collective sigh of relief when Franz Klammer gained the Downhill gold medal at the 1976 Innsbruck Winter Games could be heard not only over the Patscherkofel mountain, but all over Austria.

Strong efforts are made by Austria and Switzerland to arrive at a unified style of instruction. Pre-season there are

Young children naturally begin with the stem turn. Adults with stronger legs will miss this stage in the short ski method of instruction.

seminars and courses, which often provide bargain holidays for people prepared to be guinea-pigs, and it is hoped that the general influence will radiate out to the individual ski schools of the remotest resorts. Personal and physical resources then take over. St. Anton, for example, is to Austrian skiing what Rome is to Christianity, and its 300 ski school instructors a convocation of cardinals. Against that are hundreds of little resorts like Hinterthal, Salzburg, with 100 beds, five drag lifts and seven instructors, and, everywhere, much will depend on the individual quality of the man in charge of the instruction and his relationship with his pupils.

Plastics, fibreglass and other man-made substances have much changed the nature of skis and boots, and even controversies of the Fifties and Sixties, like the accentuated counter-rotation of the body, are now dead and buried. The modern situation may be summarised fairly briefly. The US Graduated Length Method (GLM), its modified form, the Accelerated Teaching Method (ATM), the French modification of GLM, Ski Evolutif, and Orthodox learning such as

the New Austrian System, are frequently represented as rivals, with the first three concentrating on short or shorter skis. They are in fact fruits of the same learning tree at different points of growth and exposure. A proper rivalry exists in their effectiveness with individuals, or indeed groups. Different learning systems bring people on in a shorter or longer time, with a greater facility in one or the other direction.

The Graduated Learning Method starts you with skis 100 centimetres or one metre long, the bindings set well back and the arching less pronounced, and moves you to slightly longer ones until at the end of a week or fortnight, depending on progress, you reach 150 centimetres. The ultimate aim is that you ski well on skis of any reasonable length. All the learning exercise and practice is based on parallel skiing. ATM starts you on longer skis, not less than 135 cm, and you graduate in the same way except that stemmed turns – skis in a wedge shape – are part of the curriculum. These methods have developed on the flat, groomed slopes of the USA, where snow-making machines and tractors are freely deployed, and the purpose-built French resorts. They assume a close working relationship between ski school and hire shop (rarely the case in most of continental Europe) so that skis can be exchanged without fuss. An 'expandable' ski, one that can accept attachments without destroying performance, is now being adopted. The novice instinctively realises that a shorter ski will not encourage high speeds, and

will not exact much leverage in a fall. Exponents of the shorter method claim, with justification, that the fear factor is thus much reduced or eliminated from the outset, and a relaxed individual is able to make quick progress with the variety of exercises set. Jumping, twisting and ducking feature prominently in the early stages but not ski edge setting. The snow carpet obtained by grooming assists in the knee-swivelling technique necessary for the parallel movement of short skis, but quickly bumps are seen not as enemies but aids to turning. Under controlled conditions, the skier is introduced to more demanding snow and slope variations with a longer ski appropriate to the task. Longer skis will have a pronounced arch, more flex and other qualities for the more sophisticated turns and higher speeds which at that point will be desirable.

Conventional European and American instruction, such as the Austrian National System, starts skiers on the longer ski and from the word go encourages an up and down motion together with the knee swivelling. The old plodding from snowplough to stem to stem christie to parallel is virtually a thing of the past. The modern European idea is to employ the arch and sidecut of the ski towards 'unweighted' turns.

The ski is shaped to a purpose, as Sondre Norheim early realised. In plan view it is wide at the tail, narrower in the middle and wide again at the shovel. In side aspect it is arched underneath the binding where the skier will bring most of his weight to bear. Jean Claude

Killy, asked by John Fry of *SKI* Magazine, USA, to compare his own style with that of Ingemar Stenmark, said that if a time machine were possible Stenmark would always outski him because he sits so well on the middle of the ski, not pushing his tips into the snow or pressuring the tails by sitting back. That gave him great precision because his skis were so well weighted on the snow. 'It gives him acceleration that other skiers lack because they sometimes have to push the front part of the ski into the snow to carve. He really uses the sidecut of the ski. He's able to put his weight on the entire ski, and that's something very new.'

This needs further explanation in relation to the ski shape. Standing normally, the skier will force the arch, or camber, downwards. The effect is for the ski to track in a straight line. With more force still, the ski will bow into the snow in what is known as a reverse camber. The sidecut on the inside left ski will then conduct a turn to the right, and vice versa. A skier gets his ski to turn in three main ways – by turning his knees, by skidding and by up and down motion to produce a carve. It can be, and often is, a combination.

Flat ski turning – On flat snow, and given a certain momentum, the skier simply swivels his knees in the direction he wants to go, and his flat skis, the sidecut ironed out by his weight, will turn appropriately. It is easier to do this with short or Compact skis which are less waisted and cambered, and being shorter, offer less resistance to the turning motion.

Swing or Skid turning – This derives from the old stem christie (in turn derived from the snowplough) and is the standard turn of most intermediate skiers. Rather than the weight coming down vertically on to the sidecut, the ski is pushed out sideways in a skidding motion, the tail fanning out, the weight following it a little belatedly, and the other ski hauled alongside to complete the change of direction. In an excellent description of this turn in *We Learned to Ski* (Collins), the authors say it is 'pushing outwards so that the edge bites into the show and slows him down in a regulated sideslip'.

Carved turning – This is the advanced skier's turn. Instead of the ski skidding, it changes direction entirely on its inside edge, being forced into reverse camber by speed, pressure and angulation. A pure carved turn leaves a fine, thin line in the snow where the edge has cut the surface, as opposed to a wide, fan-shaped arc where the angulated sole of the ski has pushed the snow

This gentle slope at Davos, Switzerland, is perfect for most skiers. The moguls are not too big and actually help you turn.

away. Just as it is better to steer a car without skidding, so a skier is in better control with carved turns. The sidecut on the inside edge of the left ski will help a turn to the right, and vice versa. As soon as pressure is released from the turning ski, the skier is thrown on to his other ski, instantly commissioning a turn the other way. Hence the constant speedy zigzags of so many good skiers. Their skis often seem to be parallel, indeed the term parallel skiing is widely used for this kind of technique, but in slow motion or close-up the skis may be doing a different job at different moments.

Carved turns can only be achieved by up or down unweighting. These are difficult seeming terms and often misunderstood or misused. The beginner's major problem is how to initiate a turn. To do so, he must reduce weight somehow – it is easier to move anything which does not have weight bearing down on it. If you rise on your toes on a set of bathroom scales there is a brief moment when the downward thrust sends the weight needle up a few pounds. Then it flickers to something under your actual weight as you 'take off'. That, in skiing, is up unweighting. When you come down again, helped by a small gravitational thrust, your weight briefly exceeds your actual poundage. That is downweighting. On the other hand if you are standing on the scales and suddenly bend down, thighs parallel to the ground, the needle will flicker downwards. Very briefly you are less than your actual weight, and this is down unweighting. It is while you are unweighted, up or down, that you are reducing the frictional forces between ski and snow which are opposing your turn. Then, as you come back down with distinct overweighting, the ski reverse-cambers, your weight thrust spreads along your inside ski edge, and you turn.

There are endless variants to equipment, snow condition and gradient requiring technical adjustment by the skier. At the bottom end, a novice is likely to be happier with a metre-length ski with scarcely any waisting at all. At the top end, a slalom racer will want a ski so arched and waisted that he appears to leap from sprung platforms as he dodges between the gates. As the skis bounce back from sharp reverse cambering, indeed that's what they are. Where bumps at first frighten a skier, after a while he sees them as natural aids to turning, providing he times them properly. It is a useful experience just to stand on a bump and see how readily the skis swivel. Arriving at the crest when moving, knees tucked up, then

Carved turn:

1
In this sequence the skier is executing a carved turn. Here the skier has initiated the turn by upweighting.

2
The skier is now beginning to exert pressure on the ski. This pressure will increase throughout the turn.

pushing down and turning, so safely slipping down the far side, legs extended, is an accomplishment an intermediate skier cherishes. If he can absorb a series of bumps at speed he is no longer an intermediate.

Most modern skiing, and a great deal of instruction is based on piste skiing. All classes of skier sooner or later have to cope with a fresh fall of snow or wandering into soft stuff, albeit by accident. The silk of a fresh fall, no more than 12 inches deep, on hard pack, will delight everyone experiencing the ease with which skis respond. The only barrier is in not seeing your skis. Once that purely psychological problem is overcome, ordinary piste techniques will do. Deep soft is something else. For a longer trek it helps to have a guide or instructor who knows the terrain and is aware of any gulch or trap the thick snow cover may be temporarily hiding. All too few skiers dare the obviously undangerous soft sections still inside the piste boundary poles after the narrow centre section has begun to tamp down. Here a good instructor will tell his class to advance one ski a little for the slight shock of entering the soft.

Straight runs and pulling up on a mound accustom you to the slower, dragging sensation of soft snow schus-

sing. As fear changes to pleasure at the soft hiss of the powder, your guide may encourage you to try rather more. Turning in soft snow is easier for the GLM graduates, so it is claimed, than people brought up on stem christies, for they are accustomed to turning without edging. Pushing soft snow with stem christies is certainly hard work, and requires a degree of fitness and leg strength holidaymakers may not possess. The parallel technique is to push the ski tips to the surface, allowing a little of the weight (not too much) on to the heels. The body must stay centred – it is a major error to let it slip too far back, and even worse to get too far forward. The downhill pole is planted to trigger the turn and lift the body up in the unweighting which sets off the swing. Any attempt to edge could be disastrous. You keep the skis as flat and as close together as possible and bank your body into the turn, giving yourself plenty of time to make your arc in the snow. Tighter turns will require more rapid down-up movements, in such a way that you virtually bounce from one turn into the next. The key to good powder skiing is to establish a rhythm. Once you can achieve this, the mountain is yours.

Ice terrifies most because the ski will not reverse camber as it will in

3
The turn continues, with the skier pushing his hips and knees to the inside of the turn, so setting the edge of the right ski at an angle to the snow.

4
The right knee continues to control the angle of the edge as it cuts through the snow. To the skier's right is the fine line in the snow left by a previous carved turn.

5
The turn is almost finished and the skier prepares to unweight and transfer pressure on to his left ski for the next turn. Note how the right ski has been pushed into reverse camber.

6
Instead of carving his turn, the skier is here turning by skidding on a flat ski, with little edge bite. This can be seen by the amount of snow being thrown up by the ski.

Beginner's faults:
Several faults seen in most beginners are shown here. The skier's stance is too upright, and the weight too far back. He is also putting too much weight on the inside ski of the turn, and is looking at the tips of the skis instead of looking forward to see where he is going.

softer snow and better piste conditions. You follow the advice of my Canadian friend and dig your edges in much harder when you turn. And you pray you have kept those edges sharp.

Among the European ski countries, Austria and France have set major learning trends with the Swiss in between. Italy, in spite of owning two-thirds of the Alps, and the Squadra Azzurra, with its huge success in racing skiing, has lagged behind because of a less unified approach. West Germany has a few outstanding resorts, and a modestly strong equipment industry, but principally is renowned for racers like Rosi Mittermaier and the Epple sisters and the number of weekenders and holidaymakers who pour off the autobahns into the more strictly Alpine countries. Karl Gamma of Switzerland has promoted various Inter-Ski congresses to encourage a unified European teaching method, but the others are keener to preserve a national identity. In the end the Austrian, French and Swiss methods arrive at the same point, but with varying emphases.

The French, led by Joubert and the former racer Jean Vuarnet, opposed the heavily accentuated counter-rotation of Stefan Kruckenhauser's Austrian school of the Fifties and Sixties. The French argued that the body should stay as square as possible in the turn and traverse. The Austrians, they would claim with a laugh, were losing half their instructors with slipped discs. They also taught a wider track for more stability. The Austrians subsequently reduced the angulation of upper body to legs and became less insistent on skis tight together. The French introduced jet turns, a shooting-out of the ski tips from the turns, but only a few racers, notably Patrick Russell, were capable of this, and only then with boots far higher up the calf than was practicable for tourists and day-to-day skiers.

Italy's Gustavo Thoeni offered the world something genuinely new with his passa tinto. This was a step turn often made from a low, well centred position which made him look like a speed skater in some passages, and brought him four World Cups in the years between Killy and Stenmark. Sweden, without a big Alpine tourist industry, has not been able to make much capital out of Stenmark, but he, too, has had a profound influence on international style. His exceptional strength in the lower body helps give him a calm and graceful style, but in the essentials, of staying central over his skis, for most of the time, he is an example to all.

Mogul or bump skiing:

1

The skier approaches a mogul, planning to turn on its crest.

2

Instead of letting the mogul throw him in the air, the skier absorbs the bump by bending his knees. The edges are set for the turn and the pole ready to be planted.

Deep snow skiing:

1

Whilst the snow here is not very deep, it is slightly crusted and heavy. The skier thus has had to jump out of the snow slightly to facilitate his turn.

2

Back in the snow and the skier prepares for the next turn. Note how the tips of the skis are riding out of the snow, so preventing them from 'submarining'.

3

The pole has been planted and the skis are flat, half-way through the transfer of weight and change of edge set. The skier continues to absorb the bump but prepares to extend his legs on the downhill side of the mogul.

4

The skier has extended his legs, so maintaining contact with the snow. The skis will soon be set further on edge for the continuation to the edge.

5

The right ski is well edged, the right pole ready to be planted as the skier prepares for the next mogul. Note how the knees are bent and pushed forward to control the tips.

3

The skier has started the next turn. He has planted his pole and pushed the tips further out of the snow prior to jumping them right out of the snow.

4

Out of the snow again and the skis are turned. The right pole is ready to be planted for the next turn, so maintaining the rhythm vital to good deep snow skiing.

5

The turn is finished and the skier prepares for the next turn.

Cross-country and Touring

The lure of the snow wilderness

To most, Nordic, or cross-country (X-C), skiing is amiable exercise, out in the country without spending too much cash. That is the brief, well-justified, reason for its rising popularity in the United States, Canada and various areas of the Alpine countries, Australia, New Zealand and Japan. It is easy to do for any age over about three and up to a hundred, a wonderful family activity.

A few figures are revealing. Just 12,000 pairs of Nordic skis were sold in the United States in 1967. Three years later imports were 50,000, and next year 150,000. By 1977 sales were 550,000, with a healthily expanding home-made quota, and the total of cross-country skiers around two and a half million. Although about 15 per cent of skiers were tourers, they represented only 4 per cent of ski industry sales. This is not because

of inherent meanness of ski hikers, but the basic cheapness of their activity. They don't have to pay ski lifts, they adapt quite a bit of ordinary, about-town winter clothes for touring, and the basic equipment is that much cheaper – or can be. Cross-country owes something to latent or actual puritanism, a little more to keep-fit, give-up-the-weed propaganda. In the USA, sloganising has brought 'Langlaufers live longer' or 'Get fit on a Loipe.' It is represented as the low-cost, all-natural, winter liberation movement. Like pin or skateboarding, it has made and lost adherents in the first flush of popularity, but the inherent pleasures of the activity, and the accessibility of undulating, snow-laden countryside in North America, has ensured a rising tide of popularity.

The Scandinavian countries have watched the resurgence of touring with a certain wry amusement. Downhill-only skiing, to them, is for the youngsters, a phase to be lived through, like the discovery of rock, punk and western. The true life is out into the forest or up into the vidda listening to the silence, married to nature and the hiss of skis. Some of

Out into the forests and mountains on skis . . . cross-country skiing is easy to do for any age, a wonderful family activity.

A typical view of a mass-start cross-country race. This one is the Engadine Ski Marathon in Switzerland.

The lightweight shoes of a cross-country skier are secured only at the toes, leaving the heels to lift up and down with the stride. Small prongs attached to the shoe sole near the toe fix into holes on the binding, and a sprung clamp forces the shoe welts down and into position.

the graduations of Nordic skiing are implicit here. In the Alps, or the lower mountains and hills such as the Pyrenées, Juras, Vosges and Carpathians, langlauf, ski wandern, ski touring, ski de fond, Nordic skiing or langrenn mean much the same — you ski well-marked courses, usually called loipes, of specific length and height variation, sometimes floodlit. Usual lengths are five, ten and 15 kilometres. In Scandinavia you set out on mountain and forest walks — probably a bit of both — where the intention is to discover the wilderness, to let its silence enter the soul, and its wild life brush the spirit. Paths are marked much as a bridleway might be in Britain, and close to villages and resorts there will be distinct loipes, as in the Alps. But many Scandinavians find their own path, although they will reckon to do so in groups with rucksacks containing spare warm clothing, compass and map, first aid kit, warm drink and food, whistle, matches, candle, blanket, sleeping bag and light tent. They know they must bivouac if the weather closes in and an Arctic night descends. This is cross country, as distinct from light touring, and should never be undertaken without adequate guidance and a proven measure of fitness.

Nordic equipment is simple. It is possible to spend large sums on super-lightweight plastic touring skis. Some have soles fluted like fish scales or coated

with nylon bristles or mohair. For the occasional skier, a wooden ski, narrower, lighter and longer than an Alpine Compact, may be hired, either with a permanent wax sole or more usually one requiring wax. Wax comes in two main types, one for cold snow, under zero degrees centigrade (32° Fahrenheit), the second for warm snow. As a rough guide, if the snow balls in a gloved hand it is warm, if it won't, or just blows away, it is cold. Wax is rubbed on directly, hard wax for cold snow, soft for wet. You can add soft wax to hard, but not hard to soft. If in doubt use a hard wax first. In any event give the wax a quarter-mile to take effect. A scraper and spare wax of both main types ought always to be taken on a run.

Because they have to climb as well as ski downhill, touring skiers keep pretty warm while they are moving. Their clothes can be much lighter than an Alpine skier's, but wool, cotton or any 'breathing' material is preferable. Stockings and breeches (knickers in North America) are more usually worn, with an anorak or parka over a sweatshirt of wool or cotton. Woollen hats are usual, but peak caps may be seen because they protect against twigs among the forest trails. Shoes are lightweight and comfortable. They are meant to bend at the sole, unlike Alpine boots, and have three or four small holes in the toe which accept the prongs of a touring ski bind-

Listening to the silence . . . a solitary Nordic skier on one of the loipes, or trails, at Seefeld, Austria, which hosted the 1964 and 1976 Winter Olympics Nordic competitions. Cross-country has arrived in Europe, as in North America, in a big way.

ing. The binding clamp forces the shoe welts down and attaches by a sprung toggle. The heel can rise for the long strides of touring skiing, but a serrated metal or plastic plate under the heel assists grip for turning or stopping. Unlike most Alpine skis, bindings are marked left and right.

While X-C skiing is far less demanding of practice and instruction than Alpine, and people can simply collect their equipment and set off on a short loipe, waxing can present problems. Whatever the conditions when you collect your skis, the weather can change, the snow alter, and you have to know which wax to put on, otherwise you find yourself pushing uphill three feet and sliding back two, or being left embarrassingly far behind the rest, although apparently putting in the same amount of effort.

The skilled skier has as his basic the diagonal stride, a relaxed, easy stride with a strong pushing movement and maximum glide, first with one ski then the next. Eyes focus 15 metres ahead and not on the ski tips, much as Alpine skiing. One arm plants the pole and the opposite leg pushes down and back in a horse-kicking motion, providing the push for the other leg to glide forward. Poles are swung shoulder high, and when planted just to the rear of the boot provide about 25 per cent of the force. The major force is in the kick. Once gliding finishes, a well-waxed touring ski will 'stick' as the weight comes over the top again and its anchorage is used to kick forward again. The trouble comes when the ski starts gliding back before the weight is over the top. Arms should swing close to the body, hand almost brushing the knee as it swings the pole forward. Uphill the stride is much shorter, the ski almost slapped down to create further purchase.

Double-pole pushes help momentum on downhill passages. Turns are executed much as in ice skating, with a push-off from an angled ski and the other brought alongside. At a slightly higher speed the stem turn may be used, much as in conventional Alpine skiing, the skis in a 'V', points not quite touching, and weight transferred to the left inside edge for a right turn and the right inside edge to go left. X-C skis feel less precise than Alpine, and people do fall. But with the heel not anchored and the ski not acting as a dangerous lever one instinctively relaxes. Reduced tension introduces its own cycle, and there are fewer falls on that account.

The old-time Telemark turn is a useful addition to technique, especially in soft snow, and preserves its swooping grace. One ski is slid well ahead of the other, poles parallel to the ground for stability, the knee of the rear ski in the kneeling position but not quite touching the ski surface. The forward ski is then

Into the wilds . . . Lapland represents the supreme wilderness of Europe, inhabited more by talon and paw than the ski marks of man. The call of the wild is strong in most Scandinavian hearts, but the land above the Arctic Circle is best explored when a spring sun comes to lengthen the day and put a bearable crust on the snow.

stemmed, and the skier goes round in a wide, graceful turn. It needs a bit of practice, but is well worth the perseverance.

Downhill it is usually possible to glide in tracks without fear of speeds becoming too dangerous or of the track not levelling out. It is best to follow deep tracks and not try to jump out unless there is obvious obstruction. Nor is it wise to try and stem in tracks. That only invites an outside edge catching. X-C skiing on the whole is a great deal less casualty prone than Alpine skiing. It is perfect for the Alpine ski drop-out who wants to join in the fun and get into the countryside without serious risk or loss of face.

Cross-country skiing bred famous mass-start races before the Arlberg-Kandahar was thought of. The original Birkebeiner, one of Norway's most famous races, celebrates the rescue, in 1206, of the king's son by the Birkebeiners, or birchlegs, who carried the boy 40 miles from Lillehammer across the mountains to safety. Another romance concerns the founding of the present kingdom of Sweden by Gustav Vasa in 1520. This is celebrated by the 90 kilometre (56 miles) Vasalop mass start event run since 1922 and attracting upwards of 10,000 skiers from almost every walk of life. The American Birkebeiner is now held at Telemark, Wisconsin, with 3,000 competitors or more in the 55 kilometre race. Quebec has staged the Canadian ski marathon over 160 kilometres (the longest Olympic event is 50 kilometres) since 1966 with an entry now of 4,000. Switzerland contributes the Engadine marathon. The Kandahar Club of Britain keeps the links between old and new styles with races thought up by its great pioneer, Sir Arnold Lunn, such as the Inferno, a massed start race for Alpine skiers at Mürren.

Nordic skiing, traditionally, is a combination of cross-country racing and jumping. The Nordic combination is still considered by the Scandinavian and East European snow countries to be the most prestigious event of the world Nordic Championships held alternately with the Winter Olympic Games.

Sixten Jernberg, of Sweden, has the greatest Olympic record of all cross-country skiers – four gold medals, three silver and two bronze in three Games. He retired after Innsbruck in 1964. The greatest woman, Russia's Galina Kulakova, won five world championship titles and seven Olympic medals, including three golds at Sapporo, Japan. At Innsbruck in 1976 she was deprived

of a seventh Olympic medal, a bronze, after taking a nasal spray containing a banned ingredient for a heavy cold on the eve of the 5 kilometres, in which she finished third. She was allowed to compete in the 10 kilometres and relay because it was considered a genuine mistake and won two more bronze medals.

Bill Koch, of Vermont, with his silver medal in the 1976 Olympic Games, proved a popular and persuasive exponent of cross-country skiing. In winning the 30 kilometres, however, he

You have to be a good skier to be able to ski laden down with a pack, crampons and snow shovel. This skier, Ned Gillette, is seen on Mount McKinley.

demonstrated a clear difference between the much enhanced racing techniques and ordinary cross-country. Asked after his medal if he had lived all his life in Vermont Koch gave the classic answer: 'Not yet.'

The ski tourer or mountaineer who ignores the lifts and cable-cars to seek summits and vistas that few have observed is a different animal to the piste basher. But it was he who gave alpine skiing its origins, and it is to a wilder, less-tamed form of skiing that many are turning. The cross-country explosion is part of the same urge. Ski mountaineering is an extension of ski touring, but both are invested by the same spirit. The classic high-level mountaineering route is the Haute Route from Saas Fee in Switzerland to Chamonix in France, a distance of about 120 kilometres. No one should venture into the high mountains unless reasonably fit, with a trained guide, and a map, compass, altimeter and avalanche bleeper. The simplest tour calls for study and planning, and the weather pattern taken closely into account.

Right: and above far right:
Most cross-country skiers enjoy the sport not just for the exercise but also for the scenery they will see.

Far right:
Solitude, silence and spectacular scenery are some of the joys of ski mountaineering. This group are high up in the Engadine area of Switzerland near Piz Guler.

Below:
Some of the spectacular scenery you can expect in the high mountains. This glacier lies below Mont Pourri, near Tignes in France.

Competitive Skiing

Total commitment and concentration, the goal —to be the best

The rap on the door is sharp, peremptory. There won't be another. The racer kicks off his duvet, pulls on his track suit. The room is organised mess. What you need you have to see. Travellers don't leave things in drawers. No words much to anyone. He stretches, yawns, goes through his exercise patterns. Soon his feet thump the icy undulations of a village street still slumbering. Pre-dawn air sears his lungs. A cup of coffee from a tousled waitress and down to the ski room. They're waxed and filed, taped top and bottom, a sheet of plastic sandwiched between for protection.

The adrenalin builds as the racers huddle in their cars. The mountain looms, sunlight shafting on its peaks, course in ice blue shadow. At ski lift base friends hail each other. 'Good to

To ski at 200 kph you need courage and special equipment. This kind of suit is made of a special synthetic material which reduces wind resistance and is used by all entrants to the Flying Kilometre in Cervinia.

see you.' No questions. No attitudes. Concentration builds up. Step by step they climb the slalom course. A knot gathers by a tight, tricky set of gates. No rivalries now. They talk it through. Joke a bit. Decide the best line. A few steps higher the racer stops, looks, closes his eyes, videos the course in his mind, hand weaving with his thoughts. Up top he goes into warm-up routines. A coach massages his thighs. He adjusts, readjusts goggles. 'Gate 12 rutting up.' The start coach gets his feeder messages. Some he passes on. Some he doesn't. The sun climbs. The snow's softening. The coach brings over his skis, runs sandpaper down the edges to take off the super sharpness for the softer course. The racer kicks the snow off his boots and clips into his binding. 'Number 26 prepare.' The last racer, big, formidable, so confident-seeming, is a speck down the slope. Into the gate. Careful not to touch the wand and set it off too soon. Poles now in front of the wand, weight on both skis. Look ahead. Concentrate on one thing. 'Achtung ... Bereit ... Los!' Up ... forward ... The start wand gives, the clock is ticking its hundredths of a second. But the jump technique means precious momentum already. One, two, three skating strides, and months of dedicated training and racing are on test. Will it be this time? Is this the big one? But that's for the crowd, the coach, the press. Body, mind are one. Rhythm, rhythm, and let it all hang out.

Some win by hundredths of a second, some lose. Whatever it is, World Cup, World Pro-Skiing, European Cup, NASTAR, the veterans' race, it's the adrenalin of competition, danger too, that makes a ski race something special. The four-month World Cup is the No. 1 of ski racing, the four-month 'White Circus' which has all continental Europe glued to its Saturday lunch-time TV sets for the great downhills of Val d'Isère, Kitzbuehel, Wengen, Val Gardena and the rest. Wherever it touches, in Alpine Europe, the USA, Scandinavia and Japan, the circus brings the aces, the bright young hopes, the veterans and the no-hopers. With them come a great army of managers and mechanics, press and television, invading and taking over ski villages like an occupation force. Squadra Azura Italia . . . Salomon . . . Fischer . . . Marker . . . Blizzard . . . Rossignol . . . Lange . . . Osterreicher Ski Verband . . . The cars and the vans whizz around the icy streets. The man buying postcards is Franz Klammer. The girl sipping coffee is Fabienne Serrat. The last race, the last man down, and

A clear difference exists between the much enhanced racing techniques of Nordic skiing and its amiable recreational pursuit.

The famous 'White Circus' straddles three continents, Europe, America and Asia, in its winter World Cup programme. Annemarie Moser-Proell has dominated women's racing in recent years, but the pressure is so intense among the men that most of the major stars have been specialists – Ingemar Stenmark in the Slalom, Franz Klammer in the downhill.

Above:
Alain Consincan cuts close to a gate in an American Professional parallel slalom.

·three hours later everyone has gone. For one night Val, Heavenly, Garmisch, even Kitzbuehel are like ghost towns.

World Ski Championships are sudden-death events held every four years at Alpine and Nordic centres voted upon by FIS at a congress three years earlier. It needs all that time to prepare for one week of competition in men's and women's races in three Alpine disciplines of downhill, special slalom and giant slalom. World Championships alternate in their four-year cycle with Winter Olympic Games, for which world championship medals are presented simultaneously. The World Alpine Cup has been a major season-long event since 1967 – a World Nordic Cup was instituted in 1978–79. It's the major league of international skiing with points awarded in descending quantity for best positions in each event of the three disciplines. The points system has changed almost annually as organisers have sought to stop the domination of the overall title by slalom specialists like Gustavo Thoeni and Ingemar Stenmark. Thoeni won in 1971, 72, 73 and 75, Stenmark in 1976, 77 and 78. So great was the pull of the World Cup that Austria's five times women's winner Annemarie Moser-Proell returned after a year's retirement because she missed the competition so.

Straddling three continents, and with an almost non-stop travel schedule, it is

a gruelling test of a skier's all-round stamina. Few keep it up after the age of 30, and most retire long before that. Injury takes another heavy toll, although fatalities are rare. Rewards, on the other hand, can be huge. Although almost all World Cup skiers compete in Olympic Games under heavily modified amateur rules, they are professionals in all but name, with broken-time payments from their national federations and contractual tie-ups with equipment specialists.

American world professional skiing celebrated its tenth birthday in 1978–79, competing for $600,000 on a tour calling for a WPS event almost every winter weekend. WPS is far less nationally orientated than World Cup, which is administered by FIS with sponsored backing. Bob Beattie, former US team head coach, introduced man against man slalom skiing on parallel courses, and added two or three man-made jumps at strategic intervals. In its first year total prize money was $92,500. Ten years later it was $600,000, with the format shaped for television coverage.

What the races are:

Downhill: A test of speed, bravery and stamina over a course of 2 to $2\frac{1}{2}$ miles with a minimum vertical drop of 800 metres for men and 400 for women. The terrain is carefully chosen to include bumps, rolls, gullies, sudden changes of steepness, schusses and light and shade. Most courses include a jump and a compression – a rising section to follow a sharp descent with the skier at peak speed lower down the course.

Slalom: Sometimes called special slalom to differentiate it from giant slalom, has two consecutive runs on different, though usually adjacent, courses, characterised by sharp, zigzag turns. Course length is a quarter to three-eighths of a mile (average 525

Above:
Patrick Russell followed Jean-Claude Killy's example and left the amateur World Cup for American Pro Racing.

Left:
A future Olympic star? Who knows, but skiing and racing is for all ages.

metres) on a one-in-three slope through a minimum 55 gates for men and 45 for women. Gates consist of pairs of poles. Slalom is a test of control and technique. FIS have also introduced head-to-head parallel slalom races, one such finishing the World Cup programme but not counting for points.

Giant Slalom: Originally intended as a scaled-down version of the downhill which could be staged when there was less snow and on less severe slopes, has been dominated more by slalom than downhill specialists and tests a skier's ability to hold a fast traverse and turn with good technique on courses about 1,500 metres (one mile) with a vertical drop of 450 metres (14,476 feet) through 60 to 70 gates.

FIS handicaps: Skiers are seeded according to performance, a better points ranking (the lower the figure the better) according a better start number in major races after a draw. Points are awarded in relation to the winner, a skier's two best races counting, with regular updating.

Below Olympic, World Championship and World Cup level is a wide variety of genuinely amateur racing circuits. The European Cup is more a second division of the World Cup. The Citaden circuit, on the other hand, is specifically for amateur, non-mountain racers who devote a relatively small amount of time to racing. In the USA,

One of the major gifts of US World Professional Skiing has been the development of parallel slalom – racing man against man on adjacent courses.

John Fry of *SKI* magazine introduced NASTAR, an ingenious recreational ski programme adapted from the French handicap system. In ten years it grew to the point where 81,000 separate individuals completed 220,183 courses in the season ending in 1978. The system calls on each host ski area to send a representative to an early-season pacesetting trial, where he earns a handicap in competition with top members of the world pro circuit. Back at home, the pacesetter skis each NASTAR course, and his time and handicap are calculated to determine how fast the nation's number one, or zero handicap pace-setter, would have skied that course. The per cent slower that the NASTAR racer skis that course establishes his or her handicap. Gold, silver and bronze medals are awarded according to handicap within an age and sex range. Adults earning two gold medals qualify for finals. A similar competition was introduced in 1978–79 for US cross-country skiers.

Liberation, it was a word, a style, that swept the world in the late Sixties and Seventies with very mixed consequences. No major activity could escape it, politically and sexually. Skiing was no exception, but this, in the end, was

Perfection, upside-down, in a back lay-out somersault.

one of the happier consequences. What began as a revolt against rules and regulations, and order imposed by 'dough-faced old men', as some rather sweepingly saw it, blossomed into Hot Dog. Just as Mensheviks were succeeded by Bolsheviks, and Danton by Robespierre, the revolt quickly rejected Hot Dog as a term. It had a past. It was associated with surfing. Unconventional skiing was born again as Freestyle, etymologically more exact. And great fun too.

The exact origin is confused, other than that it happened in the USA. It was a movement, not a historical fact based on a single incident, any more than the storming of the Winter Palace was the Russian revolution. Youngsters wanted to whistle down the slopes doing something other than racing each other. They wanted to leap, bound, do something different. In racing, the more a ski is off the snow the slower it goes. Surely there were ways of picking a ski off the snow and having fun? For that you needed a ski less than the seven feet of wood or composition which anchored people to the snow in the Fifties and early Sixties. Liberation was not only a mood. It was also the short ski, blunt nosed and not too beautiful, but light and flexible so

Go for it! Freestyle's motto. But even in a back lay-out spread eagle, you want to mind your tongue.

you could turn head over heels and not have it clobber you, so you could whip through the bumps or dance a pirouette or a pas de deux.

One beautiful Aspen, Colorado, morning in 1971, the first Hot Dog competition took place with one competitor zigzagging down, one turn here, six there. Another runner, just to be different, took it very slowly, a thousand and more tiny turns. It was life from a thousands cuts. Everyone loved it. The bumps and lumps of the original mogul races were not enough. Next came ballet on skis, a blood sister to figure skating, the slopes washed not only, hopefully, by sunshine, but by 'Romeo and Juliet', 'Chopsticks', 'The Sound of Music' and 'Eleanor Rigby'. The maids of the mountains were such as Suzy Chaffee, Marion Post, Genia Fuller and Joanie Teorey, zinging around with petitions, exploding masculine myths, telling presidential committees what was what.

The men were Wayne Wong, Tom Leroy, Corky Fowler, Herman Goeliner and Co., the last performing the first ever Moebius flip, a layout somersault with full twist. Aerials, a natural brother of high diving and gymnastics, at first accompanied ballet runs. But these dizzying, hell-bent manoeuvres produced such accidents that freestyle be-

'It's a whole life trip' says speed ace Steve McKinney, the world's fastest man on skis in breaking the 200 kilometre per hour barrier (124.4 mph) on the Rock of Jack run in Portillo, Chile.

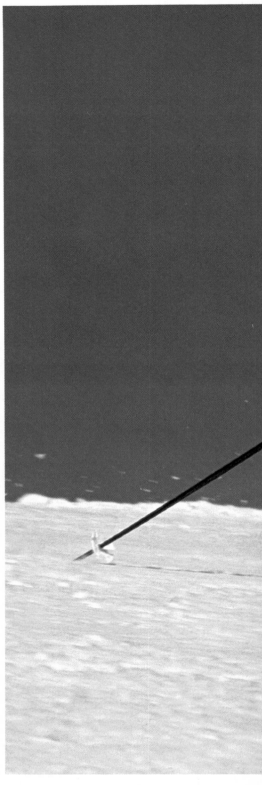

came uninsurable. The promoters, the crowds, TV and sponsors obviously loved it. But not at that price. Ballet and aerials split, the second on a much more regulated basis, with safety a major preoccupation. The somersaults became more spectacular, but only from screened competitors spending as much time on a trampoline as on a slope. At Snowbird, Utah, in 1976, Manfred Kastner, a 32-year-old Austrian, performed a triple somersault before 14,000 spectators, the freestyle equivalent to Donald Jackson, the Canadian who broke a similar ice skating barrier. Kastner also was the first to practise the deadly

dangerous, twisting, inverted jumps over a water landing. Sarah Ferguson, a British convert in the more slowly evolving European scene, built a ski slope over the family swimming pool.

A new ski form brought a new jargon and fancy, way-out garb. Daffy, Bump, Boogie, Mule Kick, Post-toastie, Spread-eagle, Wongbanger. All are aerial, ballet or mogul terms; a Daffy, for example, is a jump with one leg in front and the other behind. FIS could not ignore what was happening. A freestyle exhibition before the 1978 World Championships at Garmisch-Partenkirchen brought the house down. Essentially it developed

with a strong element of professionalism, although sponsorship came and went dizzily. Freestyle skiers, being rebels, were not always punctual for the committee meetings. Before 1977–78 there were two rival circuits and no overall sponsor for a World Cup series. Some leading North Americans, led by Scott Brooksbank, three times world champion, and John Eaves, the reigning world champion, got together with the German Fuzzi Garhammer to organise a World Cup series with events in Europe and Canada. Skiers from Britain, Sweden, France, Switzerland, Germany, Austria and even Yugoslavia, showed their

Ingemar Stenmark, Sweden's skiing superstar, as he attacks a slalom course.

Franz Klammer, from Austria, was for several years unbeatable on a downhill course. His victory in the Innsbruck Olympic downhill in 1976 was wildly celebrated throughout Austria.

commitment to freestyle, and many an ability to challenge the North Americans, who still dominate the scene. More kids freestyle the North American slopes than race. Europe has competitive amateurs, some as good or better than the professionals, but not on the same scale as the US. Essentially people freestyle for their own amusement. It is, after all, an escape from rules bondage. Any attempt to pinion it too firmly is rightly resisted. Freestyle competition will always be a kind of contradiction, and any form of judging will be as endlessly controversial as ice skating freestyle.

One great, almost incidental, gift to

skiing at large has been the short ski. If 80 per cent of vacationer skiers have been liberated by the 150 to 180 centimetre ski it is the freestylers they have mainly to thank. Manufacturers whose brand images inescapably were the 80 mph downhill aces could turn equally to the freestyle stars – and their needs were much closer to the mass of recreational skiers. 'Relax . . . hang free. . . .' From the nursery slopes of Wengen to the freestyle bowls of Aspen the message is the same, and good news for everyone.

Just as motoring has its Formula One Grand Prix, skiing has the Lauberhorn and Kitzbuehel downhills. Hillclimbs,

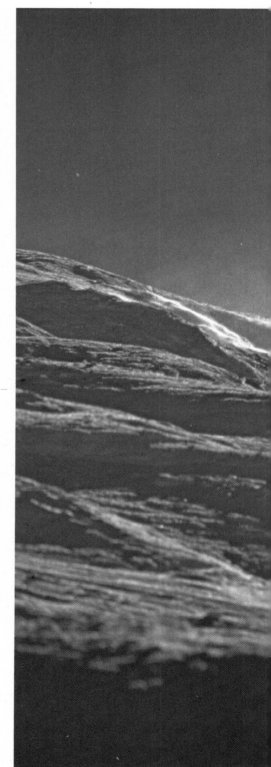

Sahara Rallies, speed tests — all have their equivalents on snow. For Craig Breedlove or Gary Gabelich there is Steve McKinney, the fastest man on skis. For Timo Makinen or Erik Carlsson, there are Yuichiro Miura, the man who skied Everest, or Sylvain Soudan, skier of the impossible. The difference is, of course, that the skier has no propulsion other than gravity, the dynamics of his own body, and his own spirit. What many of this special breed are seeking are the Ultimates. Everest's summit can be conquered not just once, but in many different ways.

Steve McKinney, a native of Squaw Valley, California, goes for the ultimate of ultimates, the fastest speed over the Flying Kilometre. On October 1, 1978, over the 50-degree slope of 'Rock of Jack', Portillo, he broke the 200 kilometre per hour barrier (124.4 mph) on a course bootpacked by Chilean soldiers. Of more than 20 taking part Mark Rowan of Canada was agonisingly close with 198.785 kph, and Ben Lindberg of Sweden next with 198.129.

McKinney's 200.222 kph beat his own record of 198 kph established earlier in the year over the Kilometro Lanciato at Cervinia, Italy. The jet men are a special breed, like creatures from

Early Freestyle was characterised by its wild exuberance. This competitor is going for broke in the Mogul event.

out of space in their wind-piercing helmets and glossy, figure-hugging suits. A special jury can disqualify anyone whose style they consider dangerous after Swiss Jean Beguelin, so anxious to keep his tuck, or doubled-up, wind-sleeked position, put his head right down and drifted off course, killing himself, in 1974. Photo-electric beams mark the jet man's passages through a 100 metre time trap to give his speed. The runners start as high as they want above the formal kilometre and its inset time trap. 'It's a whole life trip,' McKinney once said. 'It beats the hell out of drugs – it's a natural high.'

The fastest man in the world was probably travelling at 130 mph in the last few metres of the speed trap. Both Portillo and Cervinia tracks are less than 11,000 feet, so one day at a higher altitude, where thinner air creates less resistance, McKinney's record is likely

Above:
Walter Steiner shows near-perfect form and control as he flies in a jump at 60 mph.

Top:
Innsbruck, 1976, and a 90 metre jumper seems about to land in the town cemetery.

Ski jumping – one of the world's great sporting TV spectaculars, and a highspot of any Winter Olympic Games. The triple set of hills at Lahti, Finland, dominated by the 90 metre jump, have seen some of the world's best competitions. Scandinavians dominated ski jumping for decades, but Russians, East Germans, Austrians and Czechs have opened up the competition.

to be well beaten. Skis, which improve every year, are 240 centimetres with two base grooves and a low tip.

Fear is there like an adrenalin booster at the start. Then, as McKinney once wrote: 'You concentrate on what is happening. You pole off from the start, one good push. Skate. Flick the tip of your ski like the tip of a condor wing. Drop onto your knees with your instantly streamlined body, piercing the air like the missile you are, driving yourself, taut and relaxed. Vibrations begin in the tip of the ski. At first it's a subtle shimmy. Then it rapidly encompasses both skis and body. The vibration crescendo is reached at about 110 mph. Then begins the quiet side of speed skiing, with the roar of the wind just behind. Smooth. Deadly if the mind slips. The steepest part comes at 128 mph. Then the test, the flat that has been rushing up like a huge white mass.

Wham! White-black eye roll – involuntary gut-throat grunt. Thighs meet calves. Sometimes bum meets snow and gets toasted. Stand up at 100 mph into a banking turn with heavy lean. Apply brakes. Time-space warp. Back to the top, quick. Do it again, maybe better, maybe faster.'

Miura's classic descent of Everest, a feat almost matched by the cameramen who went with him, was also run for speed at high altitude. Miura had achieved 108 mph skiing Fuji to become a national hero in Japan. The 38-year-old Japanese began his descent of Everest 3,000 feet below the 28,000 foot summit on the 40 degree Lhotse face. It was no measured or pisted surface. Many saw it only as a kamikaze ritual with a doom-laden end. Miura had equipped himself with a parachute and speed skis. His descent of 6,600 feet in 2 min 20 sec represented a maximum speed of 93 mph,

but no-one who saw it on television is likely to remember it in such dry terms. Black as a beetle, darting for its life on a stark white backdrop, he was blown off course by a cyclonic gust. Those chattering skis, beyond mortal control it seemed, stayed on just long enough. He fell, hurt a hip, stopped short just before a crevasse, and survived.

Soudan, Swiss born, equally has enthralled huge television audiences with his descents over rock and snow. His three great descents were those of the Grandes Jurass on the French-Swiss border, the Eiger, which has claimed 40 deaths, and of Mount McKinley in Alaska. His ascent of the 22,000 foot peak took three weeks. His descent seven hours.

Dick Dorwarth, onetime US speed-skier and writer, wrote in *SKI* magazine: 'Why? some will ask. The answer: Why not!'

Popular Ski Locations

France:
Much of French skiing is characterised by its modern concept. The purpose-built resort, high in the mountains, with immediate access to the slopes, is a French innovation. Yet in France's two main ski areas, the Pyrenées and the Alps, the old contends with the new.

Switzerland:
Skiing and Switzerland go hand in hand. As the home of alpine skiing the traditional aspect of the sport is still noticeable; cuckoo-clock chalets abound, and the après-ski patisseries should not be missed. Switzerland's greatest attractions are the length of the runs and the breath-taking beauty of its mountains.

Italy:
With over one-third of the Alps within its borders, the range of Italian skiing is vast. This factor, combined with the country's comparatively low costs, make Italy an increasingly popular skiing country. The wide, well-manicured runs are a joy to skiers of all standards, and the easy-going atmosphere create a thoroughly enjoyable skiing vacation.

Austria:
The charm of the villages and friendliness of the Austrians has for long been the reason for people to ski in Austria. Add to this the variety of the runs, from the challenging Arlberg to the gentle Lower Austria, and you have one of the great ski countries of the world.

Japan:
Japan is a comparatively new addition to the list of ski countries; its growth has been rapid. On the whole the ski areas are much smaller than in Europe, but are equipped with many more lifts. This is to compensate for the short length of the runs and the crowds which are huge.

Australia and New Zealand:
Skiing in Australia and New Zealand has been a minority sport. It is now popular and more modern installations are being built. The slopes are shorter than is usual in Europe, and cross-country and touring are popular.

North America:
North American skiing is divided into two groups, Eastern and Western. East coast skiing is characterized by the trails cut through forests on lower mountains than in the West. There, most of the skiing takes place in the Rockies, which stretch into Canada. The light, dry powder snow of the West makes this huge region unique.

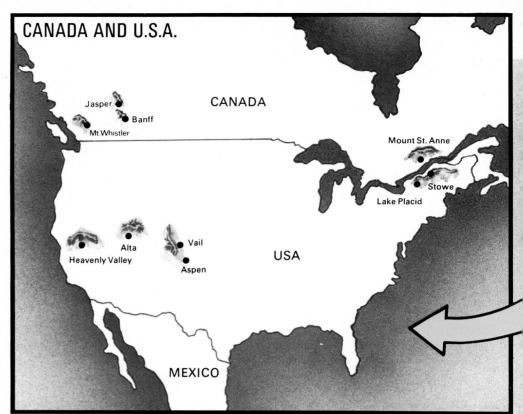

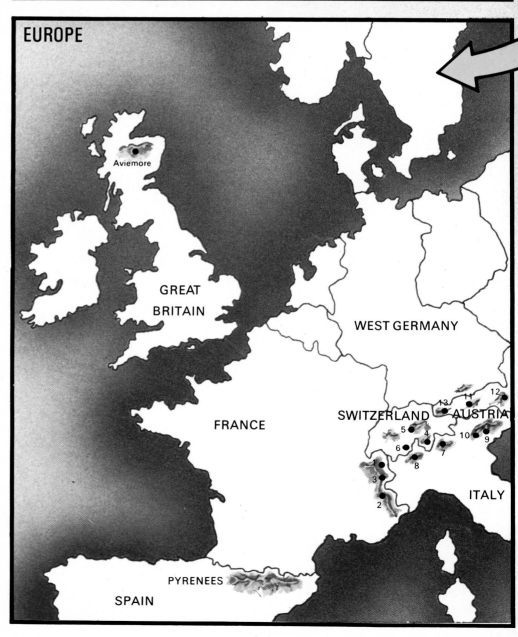